THE ANNOTATED
Casey at the Bat

E. L. Thayer (1863-1940)

THE ANNOTATED
Casey at the Bat

A Collection of Ballads about
the Mighty Casey

Edited by

Martin Gardner

THIRD, REVISED EDITION

DOVER PUBLICATIONS, INC.
New York

Bibliographical Note

This Dover Edition, first published in 1995, is the third, revised and corrected edition of *The Annotated Casey at the Bat: A Collection of Ballads about the Mighty Casey*. The first edition was published by C. N. Potter, New York, in 1967. The second edition was published in 1984 by The University of Chicago Press, Chicago. A new appendix and new illustrations have been added to the present volume.

Library of Congress Cataloging-in-Publication Data

The annotated Casey at the bat : a collection of ballads about the mighty Casey. — 3rd rev. ed. / edited by Martin Gardner.
    p.   cm.
    Reprint. Originally published: New York, C.N. Potter, 1967. With new appendix and illustrations.
    Includes original versions of the poem, Casey at the bat, by E.L. Thayer.
    Includes bibliographical references (p.).
    ISBN 0-486-28598-7 (pbk.)
    1. Thayer, Ernest Lawrence, 1863–1940—Parodies, imitations, etc. 2. Casey, Brian Kavanagh, 1859–1946—Poetry. 3. Baseball—Poetry. 4. American poetry. I. Gardner, Martin, 1914– . II. Thayer, Ernest Lawrence, 1863–1940. Casey at the bat.
PS3014.T3C332   1995
811'.04408351—dc20   95-11142
                                              CIP

Manufactured in the United States of America
Dover Publications, Inc., 31 East 2nd Street, Mineola, N.Y. 11501

For Jim Gardner, Jr.,
one of Casey's most loyal fans

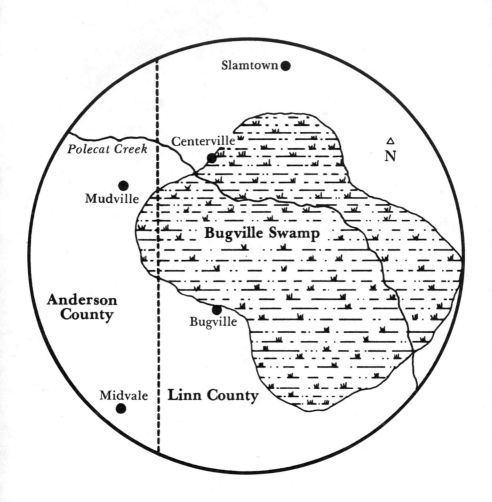

CONTENTS

LIST OF ILLUSTRATIONS

E. L. Thayer

INTRODUCTION

A MYSTERIOUS phenomenon, toward which professional critics are usually oblivious, recurs constantly in the literary history of the United States. A man or woman, with no special talent for poetry, will put together some apparently run-of-the-mill stanzas and manage to get them printed in a newspaper or magazine. The poem is read and talked about. It is reprinted here and there. People cut it out to carry in a billfold, or pin on a bulletin board, or put under the glass top of a desk, or frame and hang on a wall. Thousands memorize it. Eventually it becomes so well known that it is hard to find a literate person who hasn't read it.

The famous poem may be the only one that the author ever writes. Sometimes he composes others, but they are not published and no record of them survives. Sometimes his other poems *are* printed, but all of them are mediocre and destined for deserved oblivion. Yet that one poem, inexplicably, often to the author's own amazement, lives on to become as immortal as any poem can be on this constantly crumbling earth. When fashionable poets of the time, about whom critics have poured out reams of unstinted praise, are forgotten, the famous single poem is still going strong.

Casey at the Bat is such a poem, and its author, Ernest Lawrence Thayer, is a prize specimen of the "one-poem poet." [1] He wrote nothing else of merit. No one imagines that *Casey* is "great" in the sense that the poetry of Shakespeare or Dante is great; a comic ballad obviously must be judged by different standards. One doesn't criticize a slice of superb apple pie because it fails to taste like sirloin steak. Thayer was not even trying to write a poem in the sense that the *Ode to a Nightingale* is a poem. He was trying only to write a comic ballad, with clanking rhymes and a simple, vigorous beat, that could be read quickly, understood at once, and laughed at by any newspaper reader who knew baseball. By some miracle of creativity, in harmony with those curious laws of humor and popular taste that no one seems to think worth investigating, he managed to produce the nation's best known piece of comic verse—a ballad that began a native legend as colorful and permanent as the legend of Johnny Appleseed or Paul Bunyan and his blue ox.

It is hard now to appreciate the explosive effect that De Wolf Hopper's early recitations of *Casey* had on his audiences. We must remember that, when Hopper first began to recite the ballad, it was not widely known and the dénouement came to most of his listeners as a complete surprise. Today, everyone knows that Casey struck out. Yet the ballad bears rereading, and the more familiar its lines become, the funnier and more real Casey seems. I remember a summer when I was a boy at Camp Mishawaka in Minnesota; one of the counselors had me assigned to his canoe on a three-day boat trip, just so I could recite *Casey* for him. I must have chanted it twenty times before the trip was over. Every time I came to the line, "There was ease in Casey's manner . . ." he would almost fall out of the canoe.

This little book is my tribute to poor Casey. I have tried to tell the story behind the poem, something about its author, and, above all, to bring together for the first time as much as I could find of later material that has added to the Casey legend. Did any narrative poem ever have so many sequels and parodies? Some have not been easy to track down, and I hope that every reader who knows a Casey poem I have missed will write to me about it. None is as good as the original, some obviously are little more than doggerel. (The reader can imagine the quality of about a dozen Casey ballads I did not consider worth including.) But taken altogether, they form a substantial contribution to the Casey story. Most of them are funny, and, at the very least, the fact that they were written at all is testimony to the power of Thayer's original conception.

I must thank Anthony Ravielli for telling me about Grantland Rice's poem, *He Never Heard of Casey!*; Lee Allen, for tipping me off to Don Fairbairn's sequel and allowing me to inspect rare books and pamphlets in the library of the Baseball Museum at Cooperstown, N. Y., where he is both librarian and historian; Frank Cappio for information about King Kelly; John Shaw for some bibliographic references; Bill Bryson for locating some passages in the writings of Thomas Wolfe; David Eisendrath for some fruitful leads; George Naimark for tracking down the dates of early phonograph recordings by De Wolf Hopper; and my brother Jim for suggestions and encouragement after reading an early draft of the book. Most of all I wish to thank the niece of Casey's creator, Miss Ellen Thayer, of South Norwalk, Connecticut. She provided the photograph of her uncle that is reproduced as the frontispiece, and allowed me to look through her collection of letters from her uncle and old newspaper clippings relating to *Casey*.

MARTIN GARDNER
HASTINGS-ON-HUDSON, N.Y.

We have been shown only a fragment of their lives, beginning here, ending there, at a crucial point. I wish they didn't have to vanish in this manner. Greedily, I want to know more.

> —SANTHA RAMA RAU, writing
> about great characters of
> fiction, in *The New York Times
> Book Review*, August 1, 1965.

Two events are supremely beautiful: the strikeout and the home run. Each is a difficult and unlikely thing flawlessly achieved before your eyes.

—WILLIAM SAROYAN, in a letter to *Life*, August 23, 1954.

. . . one reason I have always loved baseball so much is that it has been not merely "the great national game," but really a part of the whole weather of our lives, of the thing that is our own, of the whole fabric, the million memories of America. For example, in the memory of almost every one of us, is there anything that can evoke spring—the first fine days of April—better than the sound of the ball smacking into the pocket of the big mitt, the sound of the bat as it hits the horsehide: for me, at any rate, and I am being literal and not rhetorical—almost everything I know about spring is in it—the first leaf, the jonquil, the maple tree, the smell of grass upon your hands and knees, the coming into flower of April. And is there anything that can tell more about an American summer than, say, the smell of the wooden bleachers in a small town baseball park, that resinous, sultry and exciting smell of old dry wood.

—THOMAS WOLFE, in a letter to Arthur Mann, included in *The Letters of Thomas Wolfe,* edited by Elizabeth Nowell, Charles Scribner's Sons, 1956, p. 722.

De Wolf Hopper

THE ANNOTATED
Casey at the Bat

One of the most humiliating defeats in the history of the New York Yankees took place on Sunday, October 6, 1963. Because a well thrown ball bounced off the wrist of first baseman Joe Pepitone, the Yanks lost the fourth straight game and the World Series to their old enemies, the former Brooklyn (but by then the Los Angeles) Dodgers. Across the top of next morning's *New York Herald Tribune* ran the headline: "The Mighty Yankees Have Struck Out." Lower on the same page another headline read: "But There's Still Joy in Mudville." (The New York Stock Exchange was holding up well under the grim news.)

Every reader of those headlines knew that they came straight out of that immortal baseball ballad, that masterpiece of humorous verse, *Casey at the Bat*. Not one in ten thousand could have named the man who wrote that poem.

His name was Ernest Lawrence Thayer. The story of how young Thayer, at the age of twenty-five and fresh out of Harvard, wrote *Casey,* and how the ballad became famous, has been told before. But it has seldom been told accurately or in much detail and, in any case, it is worth telling again.

Thayer was born in Lawrence, Massachusetts, on August 14, 1863, exactly one hundred years before the mighty Yankees made their celebrated strike out. By the time he entered Harvard, the family had moved to Worcester where Edward Davis Thayer, Ernest's well-to-do father, ran one of his several woolen mills. At Harvard, young Thayer made a brilliant record as a major in philosophy. William James was both his teacher and friend. Thayer wrote the annual Hasty Pudding play. He was a member of the Delta Kappa Epsilon fraternity and the highly exclusive Fly Club. He edited the Harvard

1

Lampoon, the college's humor magazine. Samuel E. Winslow, captain of the senior baseball team (later he became a congressman from Massachusetts), was young Thayer's best friend. During his last year at Harvard, Thayer never missed a ball game.

Another friend of Thayer's college years was the *Lampoon's* business manager, William Randolph Hearst. In 1885, when Thayer was graduated *magna cum laude*—he was Phi Beta Kappa and the Ivy orator of his class—Hearst was unceremoniously booted off the Harvard Yard. (He had a habit of playing practical jokes that no one on the faculty thought funny, such as sending chamber pots to professors, their names inscribed thereon.) Hearst's father had recently bought the ailing *San Francisco Examiner* to promote his candidacy as United States senator from California. Now that young Will was in want of something to occupy his time, the elder Hearst turned the paper over to him.

Thayer, in the meantime, after wandering around Europe with no particular goal, settled in Paris to brush up on his French. Would he consider, Hearst cabled him, returning to the United States to write a humor column for the *Examiner's* Sunday supplement? To the great annoyance of his father, who expected him to take over the American Woolen Mills someday, Thayer accepted Hearst's offer.

Thayer's contributions to the paper began in 1886. Most were unsigned, but starting in October, 1887 and continuing into December he wrote a series of ballads that ran in the Sunday editions, about every other week, under the by-line of "Phin." (At Harvard his friends had called him Phinny.) Then ill health forced him to return to Worcester. He continued for a while to send material to the *Examiner,* including one final ballad, *Casey.*[1] It appeared on Sunday, June 3, 1888, page 4, column 4, sandwiched inconspicuously between editorials on the left and a weekly column by Ambrose Bierce on the right.

No one paid much attention to *Casey*. Baseball fans in San Francisco chuckled over it and a few eastern papers reprinted it, but it could have been quickly forgotten had it not been for a sequence of improbable events. In New York City a rising young comedian and bass singer, William De Wolf Hopper, was appearing in *Prince Methusalem*, a comic opera at Wallack's Theatre, at Broadway and 30th Street. One evening (the exact date is unknown; it was probably late in 1888 or early in 1889) [2] James Mutrie's New York Giants and Pop Anson's Chicago White Stockings [3] were invited to the show as guests of the management. What could he do on stage, Hopper asked himself, for the special benefit of these men? I have just the thing, said Archibald Clavering Gunter, a novelist and friend. He took from his pocket a ragged newspaper clipping that he had cut from the *Examiner* on a recent trip to San Francisco. It was *Casey*.

This, insisted Gunter, is great. Why not memorize it and deliver it on stage? Hopper did exactly that, in the middle of the second act, with the Giants in boxes on one side of the theatre, the White Stockings in boxes on the other. This is how Hopper recalled the scene in his memoirs, *Once a Clown Always a Clown:*

When I dropped my voice to B flat, below low C, at "the multitude was awed," I remember seeing Buck Ewing's [4] gallant mustachios give a single nervous twitch. And as the house, after a moment of startled silence, grasped the anticlimactic dénouement, it shouted its glee.

They had expected, as any one does on hearing Casey for the first time, that the mighty batsman would slam the ball out of the lot, and a lesser bard would have had him do so, and thereby written merely a good sporting-page filler. The crowds do not flock into the American League parks around the circuit when the Yankees play, solely in anticipation of seeing Babe Ruth whale the ball over the centerfield fence. That is a spectacle to be enjoyed even at the expense of the home team, but there always is a chance that the Babe will strike out, a sight even more healing to sore eyes, for the Sultan of Swat can miss the third strike just as furiously as he can meet it, and the contrast between the

De Wolf Hopper

terrible threat of his swing and the futility of the result is a banquet for the malicious, which includes us all. There is no more completely satisfactory drama in literature than the fall of Humpty Dumpty.

Astonished and delighted with the way his audience responded to *Casey*, Hopper made the recitation a permanent part of his repertoire. It became his most famous bit. Wherever he went, whatever the show in which he was appearing, there were always curtain shouts for "Casey!" By his own count he recited it more than 10,000 times, experimenting with hundreds of slight variations in emphasis and gesture to keep his mind from wandering. It took him exactly five minutes and forty seconds to deliver the poem.[5]

"When my name is called upon the resurrection morning," he wrote in his memoirs, "I shall, very probably, unless some friend is there to pull the sleeve of my ascension robes, arise, clear my throat and begin: 'The outlook wasn't brilliant for the Mudville nine that day.' " The poem, declared Hopper, is the only truly great comic poem written by an American. "It is as perfect an epitome of our national game today as it was when every player drank his coffee from a mustache cup. There are one or more Caseys in every league, bush or big, and there is no day in the playing season that this same supreme tragedy, as stark as Aristophanes for the moment, does not befall on some field. It is unique in all verse in that it is not only funny and ironic, but excitingly dramatic, with the suspense built up to a perfect climax. There is no lame line among the fifty-two."

Let us pause for some moments of irony. Although Hopper was famous in his day as a comic opera star, today he is remembered for three things: 1). Hedda Hopper was the fifth of his six wives, 2). William Hopper, his only child by Hedda, is Paul Drake of the Perry Mason TV show, and 3). He was the man who recited *Casey*.

More ironic still, Gunter—who wrote thirty-nine novels including a best seller called *Mr. Barnes of New York—*

Buck Ewing, catcher for the New York Giants, whose mustache quivered when De Wolf Hopper made his first recitation of *Casey*. Note the side-buckle belt.

has found his way into terrestrial immortality only because he happened to take *Casey* out of a newspaper and pass it on to Hopper. We must not belittle this achievement. "It is easy enough to recognize a masterpiece after it has been carefully cleaned and beautifully framed and hung in a conspicuous place and certified by experts," wrote Burton Stevenson, a critic and poetry anthologist, with specific reference to Gunter and *Casey*. "But to stumble over it in a musty garret, covered with dust, to dig it out of a pile of junk and know it for a thing of beauty—only the connoisseur can do that."

Gunter was the connoisseur, but Hopper made the poem famous. All over the United States, newspapers and magazines began to reprint it. No one knew who "Phin" was. Editors either dropped the name altogether, or substituted their own or a fictitious one. Stanzas were lost. Lines got botched by printers or rewritten by editors who fancied themselves able to improve the original. Scarcely two printings of the poem were the same. In one early reprinting, by the *New York Sporting Times,* July 29, 1888, Mudville was changed to Boston and Casey's name to Kelly, in honor of Mike ("King") Kelly, a famous Chicago star who had recently been bought by the Boston team.[6]

After the banquet, at a Harvard decennial class reunion in 1895, Thayer recited *Casey* and delivered an eloquent speech, tinged with ironic humor and sadness. (It is printed, along with *Casey*, in *Harvard University, Class of 1885: Secretary's Report No. V,* 1900, pp. 88-96.) The burden of his address was that the world turns out to be not quite the bowl of cherries that a haughty Harvard undergraduate expects it to be. Surely the following passage is but a roundabout way of saying that it is easy to strike out:

We give today a wider and larger application to that happy phrase of the jury box, "extenuating circumstances." We have found that playing the game is very different from watching it played, and that splendid theories, even when accepted by the

7

combatants, are apt to be lost sight of in the confusion of active battle. We have reached an age, those of us to whom fortune has assigned a post in life's struggle, when, beaten and smashed and biffed by the lashings of the dragon's tail, we begin to appreciate that the old man was not such a damned fool after all. We saw our parents wrestling with that same dragon, and we thought, though we never spoke the thought aloud, "Why don't he hit him on the head?" Alas, comrades, we know now. We have hit the dragon on the head and we have seen the dragon smile.

From time to time various "Caseys" who actually played baseball in the late 1880's claimed to have been the inspiration for the ballad. But Thayer emphatically denied that he had had any ball player in mind for any of the men mentioned in *Casey*. When the *Syracuse Post-Standard* wrote to ask him about this, he replied with a letter that is reprinted in full in Lee Allen's entertaining book on baseball, *The Hot Stove League:*

> The verses owe their existence to my enthusiasm for college baseball, not as a player, but as a fan. . . . The poem has no basis in fact. The only Casey actually involved—I am sure about him— was not a ball player. He was a big, dour Irish lad of my high school days. While in high school, I composed and printed myself a very tiny sheet, less than two inches by three. In one issue, I ventured to gag, as we say, this Casey boy. He didn't like it and he told me so, and, as he discoursed, his big, clenched, red hands were white at the knuckles. This Casey's name never again appeared in the *Monohippic Gazette*. But I suspect the incident, many years after, suggested the title for the poem. It was a taunt thrown to the winds. God grant he never catches me.

By 1900 almost everyone in America had heard or read the poem. No one knew who had written it. For years it was attributed to William Valentine, city editor of the *Sioux City Tribune,* Iowa. One George Whitefield D'Vys, of Cambridge, actually went about proudly proclaiming himself the author; he even signed a document to this effect and had it notarized. In 1902 *A Treasury of Humorous Poetry,* edited by Frederic Lawrence Knowles, credited the poem to someone named Joseph Quinlan

Murphy. To this day no one knows who Murphy might have been, if he really existed, or why Knowles supposed he had written *Casey*.

Hopper himself did not find out who wrote the ballad until about five years after he began reciting it. One evening, having delivered the poem in a Worcester theatre, he received a note inviting him to a local club to meet *Casey's* author. "Over the details of wassail that followed," Hopper wrote later, "I will draw a veil of charity." He did disclose, however, that the club members had persuaded Thayer himself to stand up and recite *Casey*. It was, Hopper declared, the worst delivery of the poem he had ever heard. "In a sweet, dulcet Harvard whisper he [Thayer] implored Casey to murder the umpire, and gave this cry of mass animal rage all the emphasis of a caterpillar wearing rubbers crawling on a velvet carpet."

Thayer remained in Worcester for many years, doing his best to please his father by managing one of the family mills. He kept quietly to himself, studying philosophy in spare hours and reading classical literature. He was a slightly built, soft-spoken man, inclined to deafness in his middle years (he wore a hearing aid); always gracious, charming and modest. Although he dashed off four or five more comic ballads in 1896, for Hearst's *New York Journal*, he continued to have a low opinion of his verse.

"During my brief connection with the *Examiner*," Thayer once wrote, "I put out large quantities of nonsense, both prose and verse, sounding the whole newspaper gamut from advertisements to editorials. In general quality *Casey* (at least in my judgment), is neither better nor worse than much of the other stuff. Its persistent vogue is simply unaccountable, and it would be hard to say, all things considered, if it has given me more pleasure than annoyance. The constant wrangling about the authorship, from which I have tried to keep aloof, has certainly filled me with disgust." Throughout his life Thayer refused to discuss payments for reprintings of

Casey. "All I ask is never to be reminded of it again," he told one publisher. "Make it anything you wish."

Never happy with the woolly details of the family mills, Thayer finally quit working for them altogether. After a few years of travel abroad, he retired in 1912 to Santa Barbara, California. The following year—he was then fifty —he married Mrs. Rosalind Buel Hammett, a widow from St. Louis. They had no children.

Thayer remained in Santa Barbara until his death in 1940. Friends said that toward the end of his life he softened a bit in his scornful attitude toward *Casey*. By then even English professors, notably William Lyon Phelps of Yale, had hailed the poem as an authentic native masterpiece. "The psychology of the hero and the psychology of the crowd leave nothing to be desired," wrote Phelps, in *What I Like in Poetry* (Scribner's, 1934). "There is more knowledge of human nature displayed in this poem than in many of the works of the psychiatrist. Furthermore, it is a tragedy of Destiny. There is nothing so stupid as Destiny. It is a centrifugal tragedy, by which our minds are turned from the fate of Casey to the universal. For this is the curse that hangs over humanity—our ability to accomplish any feat is in inverse ratio to the intensity of our desire."

Thayer attended a class reunion at Harvard in 1935. Friends reported that he was visibly touched when he saw a classmate carrying a large banner that read: "An '85 Man Wrote *Casey!*"

Music for Thayer's poem was written by Sidney Homer and published by G. Schirmer, New York City, in 1920. (The sheet music bears the general title: *Six Cheerful Songs to Poems of American Humor.* Casey is No. 3.) Two silent movies were about Casey. The first starred Hopper himself as the mighty batsman. It was produced by Fine Arts-Triangle and released June 22, 1916. (Scenes from this film may be found in *The Triangle*, Vol. 2, June 17, 1916.) A remake, with Wallace Beery in

Wallace Beery, about to slam a homer with one hand, in Paramount's 1927 remake of an earlier motion picture version of *Casey at the Bat.*

the leading role (supported by Ford Sterling and Zasu Pitts), was released by Paramount on April 17, 1927. I can still recall Beery, bat in one hand and beer mug in the other, whacking the ball so hard that an outfielder had to mount a horse to retrieve it. An animated cartoon of the famous strike out was included in Walt Disney's 1946 release, *Make Mine Music,* with Jerry Colonna providing an off-camera recitation of Thayer's ballad. (Since 1960 this has been available as a reissued short feature from Encyclopaedia Britannica Films.) In 1953 Disney released a cartoon short called *Casey Bats Again.* It tells how Casey organized a girls' baseball team, then to save the game in a pinch, dressed like a girl and batted in the winning run.

11

The most important continuation and elaboration of the Casey story is an opera, *The Mighty Casey*, which had its world première in Hartford, Connecticut, on May 4, 1953.[7] William Schuman, who wrote the music, is now the president of New York City's Lincoln Center for the Performing Arts. He has been a baseball buff since his childhood on New York's upper west side. In his teens he seriously considered becoming a professional ball player. "Baseball was my youth," he has written. "Had I been a better catcher, I might never have become a musician." But in his early twenties his love of music won out, and by 1941 (he was then thirty-one) his *Third Symphony* lifted him into the ranks of major United States composers. From 1935 to 1961 he was president of the Juilliard School of Music, and since 1962 he has been head of Lincoln Center. Jeremy Gury, who wrote *The Mighty Casey's* libretto, has been senior vice-president and creative director of Ted Bates & Company, New York City, since 1953. Before he entered advertising he had been managing editor of *Stage Magazine*. He has written a number of childrens' books (*The Round and Round Horse, The Wonderful World of Aunt Trudy,* and others) and one play (with music by Alex North), *The Hither and Thither of Danny Dither*.

The Mighty Casey obviously is the product of two knowledgeable baseball enthusiasts. They have expanded the Casey myth with such loving insight, such full appreciation of the nuances in Thayer's ballad, that no Casey fan need hesitate to add the opera to the *Casey* canon. It is sad that Thayer did not live to see it. The details of its plot mesh so smoothly with the poem that one feels at once, "Yes, of course, that *must* have been the way it happened."

Mudville is playing Centerville for the state championship of the Inter-Urban League. In the bleachers, watching the crucial game, are two big league scouts. Casey's girl friend, Merry, knows that if Casey does well in the

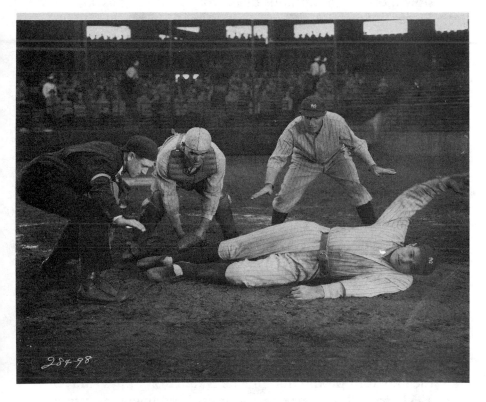

William Haines, as King Kelly, slides home
in M-G-M's 1927 movie, *Slide, Kelly, Slide!*

game he will leave Mudville forever; yet she loves him enough to offer up a prayer, in the last half of the ninth, that Flynn and Blake will not prevent her hero from coming to bat. While the fateful half is enacted in slow pantomime, the Watchman of the ball park recites Thayer's entire poem—alas, a corrupted version, but it does include two new quatrains by Gury. The final pitch is made in slow motion, an ominous drum roll beginning as soon as Fireball Snedeker (how could the Centerville pitcher have been named anything else?) releases the leather-covered sphere. Casey's tragic swing creates a monstrous wind that blows back the crowd in the grandstand, while a great whining sound from the orchestra fades off into deathlike silence. The crowd, like a Greek chorus, sings "Oh, Somewhere"—the poem's final stanza—as Casey slowly exits. Throughout the entire opera—it runs about an hour and twenty minutes—Casey speaks not a word. "We simply felt," the authors explain in their libretto, "that one so god-like should not speak. The magnificence of Casey is above mere words."

The Mighty Casey has yet to have a full-scale production in New York City. (It is not easy to put on a short opera that calls for a forty-piece orchestra and a chorus of fifty voices!) After its one performance in Hartford, there was a CBS television production of *The Mighty Casey* on the Omnibus show, March 6, 1955,[8] and it has been performed by small companies in San Francisco, Annapolis, and elsewhere. There have been several productions in baseball-loving Japan. Harold C. Schonberg, reviewing the Hartford production in *The New York Times* (May 5, 1953, page 34), spoke of the music as "lively, amusing, tongue-in-cheek." He felt that Schuman's "dry, often jerky melodic line with all its major sevenths and ninths, his austere harmonies and his rhythmic intensity," doesn't quite fit Thayer's "pleasant little fable." Can it be that the music critic of *The New York Times* is not a baseball fan? Pleasant little fable, indeed! *Casey* is neither pleasant nor little, it is tragic and titanic. Perhaps Schuman's intense music is not so inappropriate after all.

Several flimsy paperback copies of the poem, with illustrations, were printed around the turn of the century, but it was not until 1964 that *Casey* appeared in handsomely illustrated hardcover editions. I have yet to see two printings of the poem exactly alike. The Franklin Watts 1964 book comes closer to the original than any currently available printing; it follows the first version word for word except for the correction of two obvious printer's errors, and cleaner punctuation here and there.

How can one explain *Casey's* undying popularity? It is not great poetry. It was written carelessly. Parts of it are certainly doggerel. Yet it is almost impossible to read it several times without memorizing whole chunks, and there are lines so perfectly expressed, given the poem's intent, that one cannot imagine a word changed for the better. T. S. Eliot admired the ballad and even wrote a parody about a cat, *Growltiger's Last Stand,* in which many of Thayer's lines are echoed.[9]

The poem's secret can be found, of all places, in the autobiography of George Santayana, another famous Harvard philosopher. Santayana was one of Thayer's associate editors on the *Lampoon.* "The man who gave the tone to the *Lampoon* at that time," Santayana writes, "was Ernest Thayer. . . . He seemed a man apart, and his wit was not so much jocular as Mercutio-like, curious and whimsical, as if he saw the broken edges of things that appear whole. There was some obscurity in his play with words, and a feeling (which I shared) that the absurd side of things is pathetic. Probably nothing in his later performance may bear out what I have just said of him, because American life was then becoming unfavorable to idiosyncrasies of any sort, and the current smoothed and rounded out all the odd pebbles." [10]

But Santayana was wrong. One thing *did* bear this out, and that was *Casey*. It is precisely the blend of the absurd

15

and the tragic that lies at the heart of Thayer's remarkable poem. Casey is the giant of baseball who, at his moment of potential triumph, strikes out. A pathetic figure, yet comic because of the supreme arrogance and confidence with which he approached the plate.

> There was ease in Casey's manner as he stepped into his
> place;
> There was pride in Casey's bearing and a smile on Casey's
> face.
> And when, responding to the cheers, he lightly doffed his
> hat,
> No stranger in the crowd could doubt 'twas Casey at the
> bat.

It is the shock of contrast between this beautiful build-up and the final fizzle that produces the poem's explosion point. The story of Casey has become an American myth because Casey is the incomparable, towering symbol of the great and glorious poop-out.

One might argue that Thayer, with his extraordinary beginning at Harvard, his friendship with James and Santayana, his lifelong immersion in philosophy and the great books, was himself something of a Casey. In later years his friends were constantly urging him to write, but he would always shake his head and reply, "I have nothing to say." Not until just before his death, at the age of seventy-seven, did he make an attempt to put some serious thoughts on paper. Then it was too late. *"Now* I have something to say," he said, "and I am too weak to say it." [11]

But posterity's judgments are hard to anticipate. Thayer's writing career was no strike out. He swatted one magnificent home run, *Casey at the Bat;* and as long as baseball is played on this old earth, on Mudville, the air will be shattered over and over again by the force of Casey's blow.

"The mighty Casey."
A painting by Paul Nonnast.

The scene is instant, whole and wonderful. In its beauty and design that vision of the soaring stands, the pattern of forty thousand empetalled faces, the velvet and unalterable geometry of the playing field, and the small lean figures of the players, set there, lonely, tense and waiting in their places, bright, desperate solitary atoms encircled by that huge wall of nameless faces, is incredible. And more than anything, it is the light, the miracle of light and shade and color—the crisp, blue light that swiftly slants out from the soaring stands and, deepening to violet, begins to march across the velvet field and towards the pitcher's box, that gives the thing its single and incomparable beauty.

The batter stands swinging his bat and grimly waiting at the plate, crouched, tense, the catcher, crouched, the umpire, bent, hands clasped behind his back, and peering forward. All of them are set now in the cold blue of that slanting shadow, except the pitcher who stands out there all alone, calm, desperate, and forsaken in his isolation, with the gold-red swiftly fading light upon him, his figure legible with all the resolution, despair and lonely dignity which that slanting, somehow fatal light can give him.

—THOMAS WOLFE, *Of Time and the River,*
Chapter XIX.

To show you how low-brow I am
    I sadly must admit
When reading Mary and her Lamb
    I wish I'd written it;
I'd rather, I can tell you flat,
    When for Parnassus bound,
Have authored *Casey at the Bat*
    Than odes of Ezra Pound.

—ROBERT W. SERVICE, "LOW-BROW."

1. CASEY AT THE BAT

by Ernest L. Thayer

First printing.

THIS is the original version of *Casey*—word for word, comma for comma—exactly as it appeared in the fourth column on the fourth page of the *San Francisco Examiner,* Sunday morning, June 3, 1888.

CASEY AT THE BAT

A Ballad of the Republic, Sung in the Year 1888

The outlook wasn't brilliant for the Mudville nine that
    day; [1]
The score stood four to two with but one inning more to
    play.
And then when Cooney [2] died at first, and Barrows [3] did
    the same,
A sickly silence fell upon the patrons of the game.

A straggling few got up to go in deep despair. The rest
Clung to that hope which springs eternal in the human
    breast;[4]
They thought if only Casey [5] could but get a whack at
    that—
We'd put up even money now with Casey at the bat.

But Flynn [6] preceded Casey, as did also Jimmy Blake,[7]
And the former was a lulu [8] and the latter was a cake; [9]
So upon that stricken multitude grim melancholy sat,
For there seemed but little chance of Casey's getting to the
    bat.

But Flynn let drive a single, to the wonderment of all,
And Blake, the much despis-ed, tore the cover off the
    ball; [10]
And when the dust had lifted, and the men[11] saw what
    had occurred,
There was Johnnie [12] safe at second and Flynn a-hugging
    third.

Then from 5,000 throats and more there rose a lusty yell;
It rumbled through the valley, it rattled in the dell;
It knocked upon the mountain and recoiled upon the flat,
For Casey, mighty Casey, was advancing to the bat.

There was ease in Casey's manner as he stepped into his
    place;
There was pride in Casey's bearing and a smile on Casey's
    face.
And when, responding to the cheers, he lightly doffed his
    hat,
No stranger in the crowd could doubt 'twas Casey at the
    bat.

Ten thousand eyes were on him as he rubbed his hands
with dirt;
Five thousand tongues applauded when he wiped them
on his shirt.
Then while the writhing pitcher [13] ground the ball into
his hip,
Defiance gleamed in Casey's eye, a sneer curled Casey's
lip.[14]

And now the leather-covered sphere came hurtling
through the air,
And Casey stood a-watching it in haughty grandeur there.
Close by the sturdy batsman the ball unheeded sped—
"That ain't my style," said Casey. "Strike one," the
umpire[15] said.

From the benches, black with people, there went up a
muffled roar,
Like the beating of the storm-waves on a stern and distant
shore.[16]
"Kill him! Kill the umpire!" shouted some one on the
stand;
And it's likely they'd have killed him had not Casey raised
his hand.

With a smile of Christian charity great Casey's visage
shone;
He stilled the rising tumult; he bade the game go on;
He signaled to the pitcher, and once more the spheroid
flew;
But Casey still ignored it, and the umpire said, "Strike
two."

"Fraud!" cried the maddened thousands, and echo answered fraud;
But one scornful look from Casey and the audience was
awed.
They saw his face grow stern and cold, they saw his
muscles strain,
And they knew that Casey wouldn't let that ball go by
again.[17]

The sneer is gone from Casey's lip, his teeth are clenched
in hate;
He pounds with cruel violence his bat upon the plate.
And now the pitcher holds the ball, and now he lets it go,
And now the air is shattered by the force of Casey's blow.

Oh, somewhere in this favored land the sun is shining bright;
The band is playing somewhere, and somewhere hearts are light,
And somewhere men are laughing, and somewhere children shout;
But there is no joy in Mudville [18]—mighty Casey has struck out.[19]

"Mighty Casey has struck out."
A painting by Albert Dorne.

2. CASEY AT THE BAT

by Ernest L. Thayer

An early corrupted version.

HUNDREDS of versions of *Casey* have been printed, and seldom have two been exactly alike. The following version, from Frederic Lawrence Knowles's *Treasury of Humorous Poetry,* 1902, pages 297-299, was the first to appear in an anthology of humorous verse. It introduced many changes—the opening line, for example, and Barrows to Burrows—that persisted through most later printings of the ballad. Knowles attributed the poem to one Joseph Quinlan Murphy.

CASEY AT THE BAT

It looked extremely rocky for the Mudville nine that day,
The score stood four to six with but an inning left to play.
And so, when Cooney died at first, and Burrows did the
    same,
A pallor wreathed the features of the patrons of the game.

A straggling few got up to go, leaving there the rest,
With that hope which springs eternal within the human
    breast.
For they thought if only Casey could get a whack at that,
They'd put up even money with Casey at the bat.

But Flynn preceded Casey, and likewise so did Blake,
And the former was a pudding [1] and the latter was a fake;
So on that striken multitude a death-like silence sat.
For there seemed but little chance of Casey's getting to the
    bat.

But Flynn let drive a single to the wonderment of all,
And the much despisèd Blakey tore the cover off the ball,
And when the dust had lifted and they saw what had
    occurred,
There was Blakey safe on second, and Flynn a-hugging
    third.

Then from the gladdened multitude went up a joyous
    yell,
It bounded from the moutain top and rattled in the dell,
It struck upon the hillside, and rebounded on the flat,
For Casey, mighty Casey, was advancing to the bat.

There was ease in Casey's manner as he stepped into his
    place,
There was pride in Casey's bearing and a smile on Casey's
    face,
And when responding to the cheers he lightly doffed his
    hat.
No stranger in the crowd could doubt, 'twas Casey at the
    bat.

Ten thousand eyes were on him as he rubbed his hands
    with dirt,

Five thousand tongues applauded as he wiped them on
his shirt;
And while the writhing pitcher ground the ball into his
hip—
Defiance gleamed from Casey's eye—a sneer curled Casey's
lip.

And now the leather-covered sphere came hurtling
through the air,
And Casey stood a-watching it in haughty grandeur there;
Close by the sturdy batsman the ball unheeded sped—
"That hain't my style," said Casey—"Strike one," the
umpire said.

From the bleachers black with people there rose a sullen
roar,
Like the beating of the storm waves on a stern and distant
shore,
"Kill him! kill the Umpire!" shouted some one from the
stand—
And it's likely they'd have done it had not Casey raised his
hand.

With a smile of Christian charity great Casey's visage
shone,
He stilled the rising tumult and he bade the game go on;
He signalled to the pitcher and again the spheroid flew,
But Casey still ignored it and the Umpire said "Strike
two."

"Fraud!" yelled the maddened thousands, and the echo
answered "Fraud."
But one scornful look from Casey and the audience was
awed;
They saw his face grow stern and cold; they saw his muscles strain,
And they knew that Casey would not let that ball go by
again.

The sneer is gone from Casey's lip; his teeth are clenched
with hate,
He pounds with cruel violence his bat upon the plate;
And now the pitcher holds the ball, and now he lets it go,
And now the air is shattered by the force of Casey's blow.

Oh! somewhere in this favored land the sun is shining bright,
The band is playing somewhere, and somewhere hearts are light,
And somewhere men are laughing, and somewhere children shout;
But there is no joy in Mudville—mighty Casey has "Struck Out."

3. *CASEY AT THE BAT*

by Ernest L. Thayer

Revised version.

THE first authorized revision of *Casey*, as well as the first to appear in a hardcover book, is on pages 88-90 of *Harvard University, Class of 1885: Secretary's Report No. V* (1900). At a class reunion dinner, in June, 1895, Thayer recited his ballad, altering it slightly, here and there, from the original. This first revised version is substantially the same, aside from punctuation differences, as the version he gave to *The Bookman* for its January, 1909, issue (page 434). When Burton Stevenson reprinted *Casey* in his *Famous Single Poems* (1923), Thayer requested that the *Bookman* version be used, and it is this version that is reprinted here. Stevenson's opinion was that it is not as good as the 1888 original, having lost in the polishing some of its earlier "spontaneity" and "vim." Nevertheless, it is the last known revision of the ballad by Thayer himself, and unless a later one turns up, it must be considered the final "authorized" version. I have indicated in notes the principal spots where Thayer's earlier revision differs from both this and the original.

CASEY AT THE BAT

The outlook wasn't brilliant for the Mudville nine that
    day:
The score stood four to two, with but one inning more to
    play,
And then [1] when Cooney died at first, and Barrows did
    the same,
A pall-like silence fell upon the patrons of the game.

A straggling few got up to go in deep despair.[2] The rest
Clung to that hope which springs eternal in the human
    breast; [3]
They thought, "If only Casey could but get a whack at
    that—[4]
We'd put up even money now, with Casey at the bat."

But Flynn preceded Casey, as did also Jimmy Blake,
And the former was a hoodoo,[5] while the latter was a cake;
So upon that stricken multitude grim melancholy sat,
For there seemed but little chance of Casey getting to the
    bat.

But Flynn let drive a single, to the wonderment of all,
And Blake, the much despisèd, tore the cover off the ball;
And when the dust had lifted, and men saw what had
    occurred,
There was Jimmy safe at second and Flynn a-hugging
    third.

Then from five thousand throats and more there rose a
    lusty yell;
It rumbled through the valley, it rattled in the dell;
It pounded on the mountain and recoiled upon the flat,
For Casey, mighty Casey, was advancing to the bat.

There was ease in Casey's manner as he stepped into his
    place;
There was pride in Casey's bearing and a smile lit Casey's
    face.
And when, responding to the cheers, he lightly doffed his
    hat,
No stranger in the crowd could doubt 'twas Casey at the
    bat.

Ten thousand eyes were on him as he rubbed his hands with dirt;
Five thousand tongues applauded when he wiped them on his shirt;
Then while the writhing pitcher ground the ball into his hip,
Defiance flashed in Casey's eye, a sneer curled Casey's lip.

And now the leather-covered sphere came hurtling through the air,
And Casey stood a-watching it in haughty grandeur there.
Close by the sturdy batsman the ball unheeded sped—
"That ain't my style," [6] said Casey. "Strike one!" the umpire said.

From the benches, black with people, there went up a muffled roar,
Like the beating of the storm-waves on a stern and distant shore; [7]
"Kill him! Kill the umpire!" [8] shouted some one on the stand;
And it's likely they'd have killed him had not Casey raised his hand.

With a smile of Christian charity great Casey's visage shone;
He stilled the rising tumult; he bade the game go on;
He signaled to the pitcher, and once more [9] the dun sphere flew;
But Casey still ignored it, and the umpire said, "Strike two!"

"Fraud!" cried the maddened thousands, and echo answered "Fraud!"
But one scornful look from Casey and the audience was awed.
They saw his face grow stern and cold, they saw his muscles strain,
And they knew that Casey wouldn't let that ball go by again.

The sneer has fled [10] from Casey's lip, his teeth are clenched in hate;
He pounds with cruel violence his bat upon the plate.

34

And now the pitcher holds the ball, and now he lets it go,
And now the air is shattered by the force of Casey's blow.

Oh, somewhere in this favored land the sun is shining
    bright;
The band is playing somewhere, and somewhere hearts are
    light,
And somewhere men are laughing, and little children
    shout;
But there is no joy in Mudville—great Casey has struck
    out.

4. CASEY'S REVENGE

by Grantland Rice

First book printing.

It was inevitable, in the light of Casey's charismatic character and dreadful downfall, that other versifiers would provide him with a second chance. The best of many such sequels is *Casey's Revenge,* written by Grantland Rice in 1906, when he was twenty-six and sports editor of the *Nashville Tennessean.* Later he became sports editor of the *New York Herald Tribune* and the country's best known, best loved sports writer. I do not know where *Casey's Revenge* was first published. The earliest printing I could find was in a quarterly magazine called *The Speaker* (Vol. 2, No. 3, June, 1907, pages 205-207) where it was credited to one James Wilson. perhaps the pseudonym Rice had previously used.

Many later printings of the poem bear the Wilson name, including a cut version (three stanzas are missing) that appears in Hazel Felleman's *Best Loved Poems of the American People* and Ralph Woods's *Second Treasury of the Familiar.* One anthologist (Charles O'Brien Kennedy, in *A Treasury of American Ballads*) asserts that it was written by Thayer himself and printed in the *San Francisco Examiner* a month after the original ballad! There is no doubt, however, about Rice's authorship. He included it in his now-rare little book, *Base-Ball Ballads,* published by The Tennessean Company, Nashville, 1910. It is this version which follows.

CASEY'S REVENGE

There were saddened hearts in Mudville for a week or
    even more;
There were muttered oaths and curses—every fan in town
    was sore.
"Just think," said one, "how soft it looked with Casey at
    the bat,
And then to think he'd go and spring a bush league trick
    like that!"

All his past fame was forgotten—he was now a hopeless
    "shine." [1]
They called him "Strike-Out Casey," from the mayor
    down the line;
And as he came to bat each day his bosom heaved a sigh,
While a look of hopeless fury shone in mighty Casey's eye.

He pondered in the days gone by that he had been their
    king,
That when he strolled up to the plate they made the
    welkin ring;
But now his nerve had vanished, for when he heard them
    hoot
He "fanned" or "popped out" daily, like some minor
    league recruit.

He soon began to sulk and loaf, his batting eye went
    lame;
No home runs on the score card now were chalked against
    his name;
The fans without exception gave the manager no peace,
For one and all kept clamoring for Casey's quick release.

The Mudville squad began to slump, the team was in the
    air;
Their playing went from bad to worse—nobody seemed
    to care.
"Back to the woods with Casey!" was the cry from
    Rooters' Row.
"Get some one who can hit the ball, and let that big
    dub go!"

The lane is long, some one has said, that never turns
again,
And Fate, though fickle, often gives another chance to
men;
And Casey smiled; his rugged face no longer wore a
frown—
The pitcher who had started all the trouble came to town.

All Mudville had assembled—ten thousand fans had come
To see the twirler who had put big Casey on the bum;
And when he stepped into the box, the multitude went
wild;
He doffed his cap in proud disdain, but Casey only
smiled.

"Play ball!" the umpire's voice rang out, and then the
game began.
But in that throng of thousands there was not a single fan
Who thought that Mudville had a chance, and with the
setting sun
Their hopes sank low—the rival team was leading "four
to one."

The last half of the ninth came round, with no change in
the score;
But when the first man up hit safe, the crowd began to
roar;
The din increased, the echo of ten thousand shouts was
heard
When the pitcher hit the second ² and gave "four balls"
to the third.

Three men on base—nobody out—three runs to tie the
game!
A triple meant the highest niche in Mudville's hall of
fame;
But here the rally ended and the gloom was deep as night,
When the fourth one "fouled to catcher" and the fifth
"flew out to right."

A dismal groan in chorus came; a scowl was on each face
When Casey walked up, bat in hand, and slowly took his
place;

His bloodshot eyes in fury gleamed, his teeth were clenched in hate;
He gave his cap a vicious hook and pounded on the plate.

But fame is fleeting as the wind and glory fades away;
There were no wild and woolly cheers, no glad acclaim this day;
They hissed and groaned and hooted as they clamored: "Strike him out!"
But Casey gave no outward sign that he had heard this shout.

The pitcher smiled and cut one loose—across the plate it sped;
Another hiss, another groan. "Strike one!" the umpire said.
Zip! Like a shot the second curve broke just below the knee.
"Strike two!" the umpire roared aloud; but Casey made no plea.

No roasting for the umpire now—his was an easy lot;
But here the pitcher whirled again—was that a rifle shot?
A whack, a crack, and out through the space the leather pellet flew,
A blot against the distant sky, a speck against the blue.

Above the fence in center field in rapid whirling flight
The sphere sailed on—the blot grew dim and then was lost to sight.
Ten thousand hats were thrown in air, ten thousand threw a fit,
But no one ever found the ball that mighty Casey hit.

O, somewhere in this favored land dark clouds may hide the sun,
And somewhere bands no longer play and children have no fun!
And somewhere over blighted lives there hangs a heavy pall,
But Mudville hearts are happy now, *for Casey hit the ball.*

5. *CASEY'S REVENGE*

by Grantland Rice

Revised version.

LIKE Thayer, Rice later revised his ballad about Casey without noticeably improving it. The following version is reprinted from Rice's book of poems, *Only the Brave*, 1941, with the permission of the publisher, A. S. Barnes and Company.

POSTSCRIPT

GENE MURDOCK, of Marietta, Ohio, sent me a copy of page 62 of a magazine he could not identify; probably a sports publication of the 1940s. It has under Rice's byline, a version of *Casey's Revenge* that differs in many lines from either of the two versions I give, and contains two new stanzas.

The last two lines of stanza 13 read:

> They hissed and groaned and hooted as they hollered, "strike
>   him out!"
> But Casey gave no outward sign that he had heard this shout.

Then comes the following stanza:

> Here was his chance—and something snapped in Casey's tor-
>   tured soul;
> He felt his muscles bulge and strain, he felt the red blood roll;
> He felt the crowd back on his head—he felt the touch of luck—
> "Come on, you mug, and lay one through—but don't forget
>   to duck."

Instead of the final stanza of the early version ("O, some-where . . .") the following stanza closes the poem:

> Each town must have its hero, though it turns at times to mock;
> It doesn't matter who he is, so long as he can sock;
> When I asked Casey how he felt—he looked up from his cup—
> "That Thayer made a bum o' me—I had to show him up."

CASEY'S REVENGE

(Revised and reedited in the wake of E. L. Thayer's
slugless sonata of a cracked dream.)

There were broken hearts in Mudville for a week or even
more.
There were muttered, throbbing curses—every fan in town
was sore.
"Just think," said one, "how soft it looked with Casey at
the bat—
And then to think he'd go and spring a bush-league trick
like that."

All his past fame was forgotten—he was now a hopeless
punk,[1]
They called him "Strike-out Casey"—both the sober and
the drunk.
And as he came to bat each day his stout lungs heaved a
sigh,
While a look of hopeless fury shone in mighty Casey's
eye.

He pondered on the days gone by that he had been their
king—
That when he strolled up to the plate they made the
welkin ring.
Their echoes socked the mountainside and rolled across
the flat
As Casey—mighty Casey—swaggered Ruth-like up to bat.

He soon began to sulk and loaf—his batting eye went
lame.
No home runs on the score card now were chalked against
his name.
And the fans without exception gave the manager no
peace,
As one and all kept clamoring for Casey's quick release.

The Mudville team began to slump—the clucks [2] were in
the air.
Their playing went from bad to worse—nobody seemed
to care.

"Back to the bush with Casey!" was the cry from Rooters'
   Row.
"Get someone who can hit the ball and let that big mug
   go!"

The sneer was gone from Casey's lips—the smile had left
   his face.
Defiance, known to vanished days, no longer held its
   place.
For men are made by deed on deed, by grinding mile on
   mile,
But men are broken in a flash when Fortune shifts her
   smile.

The lane is long, someone has said, that never turns
   again,
And fate, though fickle, often slips another chance to men.
In Casey's eyes a new light shone—his forehead lost its
   frown—
The pitcher who had fanned him in the pinches ³ came to
   town.

All Mudville had assembled there—ten thousand fans
   had come
To cheer the twirler who had turned their king into a
   bum.
And when he stepped into the box the raving mob went
   wild.
He doffed his cap in proud disdain—but Casey only
   smiled.

"Play ball"—the umpire's call went out—and then the
   game began,
But in that mob of sorrow there was not a single fan
Who thought that Mudville had a chance—and with the
   setting sun
Their hopes sank low—the rival team was leading four
   to one.

The last half of the ninth came 'round—with no change
   in the score.
But when the first man up hit safe the crowd began to
   roar.

The din increased—the echo of ten thousand throats was heard
As the wobbling pitcher packed the paths from first around to third.

Three men on base—nobody out—three runs to tie the game!
A triple meant the highest niche in Mudville's hall of fame.
But here the rally ended and the gloom was deep as night
As the fourth one fouled to catcher and the fifth flew out to right.

A dismal groan in chorus came—a scowl was on each face,
As Casey walked up, bat in hand, and grimly took his place.
His bloodshot eyes in fury gleamed, his teeth were clenched in hate,
He gave his cap a vicious tug and pounded on the plate.

But fame is fleeting as the wind—and glory fades away.
There were no wild and woolly cheers—no glad acclaim this day.
They called for Tony [4] or for Pete [5]—for bat boy or for clown—
For anyone—except the punk who threw their city down.

The pitcher grinned—and cut one loose—across the plate it sped.
Another hiss—another groan—"Strike one," the umpire said.
Zip—like a shot the second curve broke just above his knee—
"Strike two," the umpire called again—but Casey made no plea.

No roasting for the umpire now—his was an easy lot—
But here the pitcher whirled again—was that a rifle shot?
A crash—a smash—and out through space the leather pellet flew,
A blot against the distant sky—a speck against the blue.

Above the fence in center field in rapid whirling flight
The ball sailed on—the blot grew dim—and then was lost
  to sight,
Ten thousand hats were thrown in air—ten thousand
  threw a fit.
But no one ever found the ball that mighty Casey hit.

*   *   *   *   *

L'envoi

There is no sequel to this plot—except in Mudville's
  square
The bronze bust of a patriot—arms crossed—is planted
  there.
His cap is cocked above one eye—and from his rugged
  face
The sneer still curls above the crowd—across the market-
  place.

And underneath, in solid bronze, these words are graved
  in flame—
"Here is a man who rose and fell—and rose again to
  fame—
He blew a big one in the pinch—but facing jeering
  throngs
He came through Hell to scramble back—and prove a
  champ belongs."

6. *MUDVILLE'S FATE*

by Grantland Rice

ALMOST no one today remembers Rice's second sequel, *Mudville's Fate,* which appeared in *Base-Ball Ballads* along with *Casey's Revenge.* Rice introduces it by saying that it depicts "the sad finish of Mudville after the celebrated Son of Swat put the township on the blink by whiffing in the championship game, thus wiping out all interest in a hitherto thriving baseball center." The poem, he adds, is rivaled only by Goldsmith's *Deserted Village.* For the meaning of "whiffing" see Note 2.

A slightly different version of the poem appeared in *Sporting Life* (December 27, 1913), and is reprinted in Eugene Murdock's *Mighty Casey* (Greenwood, 1984, page 118).

MUDVILLE'S FATE

I wandered back to Mudville, Tom, where you and I
    were boys,
And where we drew in days gone by our fill of childish
    joys;
Alas! the town's deserted now, and only rank weeds grow
Where mighty Casey fanned the air just twenty years ago.

Remember Billy Woodson's place, where, in the evening's
    shade,
The bunch would gather and discuss the home runs Casey
    made?
Dog fennel [1] now grows thick around that "joint" we used
    to know,
Before old Casey whiffed [2] the breeze some twenty years
    ago.

The grandstand, too, has been torn down; no bleachers
    met my gaze
Where you and I were wont to sit in happy bygone days;
The peanuts which we fumbled there have sprouted in
    a row
Where mighty Casey swung in vain just twenty years
    ago.

O how we used to cheer him, Tom, each time he came
    to bat!
And how we held our breath in awe when on the plate
    he spat;
And when he landed on the ball, how loud we yelped!
    But O
How loud we cursed when he struck out some twenty years
    ago!

The diamond is a corn patch now; the outfield's over-
    grown
With pumpkin vines and weedy plots; the rooters all
    have flown—
They couldn't bear to live on there, for nothing was the
    same
Where they had been so happy once before that fatal
    game.

The village band disbanded soon; the mayor, too, resigned.
The council even jumped its graft, and in seclusion pined;
The marshal caught the next train out, and those we
used to know
Began to leave in flocks and droves some twenty years
ago.

For after Casey fanned that day the citizens all left,
And one by one they sought new lands, heartbroken and
bereft;
The joyous shout no more rang out of children at their
play;
The village blacksmith closed his shop; the druggist
moved away.[3]

Alas for Mudville's vanished pomp when mighty Casey
reigned!
Her grandeur has departed now; her glory's long since
waned.
Her place upon the map is lost, and no one seems to
care
A whit about the old town now since Casey biffed [4] the air.

7. THE MAN WHO PLAYED WITH ANSON ON THE OLD CHICAGO TEAM

by Grantland Rice

ANOTHER now-forgotten Casey poem also appeared in Rice's *Base-Ball Ballads*. It is a parody, as Rice points out, of Eugene Field's *The Man Who Worked with Dana on the Noo York Sun*. At first one is inclined to think that it tells the inside story of why Casey struck out, but internal evidence reveals it to be pure fabrication (*i.e.,* Casey here comes to bat when the bases are loaded, but we know from Thayer's more trustworthy account that there were only two men, Flynn and Blake, on base). The poem is amusing, but of course it has nothing to do with the real Casey.

THE MAN WHO PLAYED WITH ANSON
ON THE OLD CHICAGO TEAM

Thar showed up out in Mudville in the spring of '83
A feller evidently just recoverin' from a spree.
He said his name was Casey, and he wuz a sight to view
As he walked into the ball park, and inquired for work
  to do.
Thar wuzn't any openin', for you should understand
That wuz the time when Mudville had a bunch of stars
  on hand;
But the stranger lingered, tellin' Mickey Nolan and the
  rest
What an all-fired battin' av'rage he possessed when at
  his best,
Till finally he stated, quite by chance, as it would seem,
That he had played with Anson [1] on the old Chicago
  team.

Wal, that was quite another thing; we owned that any
  cuss
Who'd played with old Pop Anson must be good enough
  for us;
So we took Casey at his word and signed him while we
  could,
Well knowin' if we didn't that some other ball club
  would,
For Kankakee [2] wuz lookin' round for people that could
  play,
And Pikeville [3] wouldn't overlook this feller any day;
And we give him quite a contract, tho' it made the others
  swear,
Sayin' we had done 'em dirty and it wuzn't on the square;
But we laid back and cackled, for the pennant warn't no
  dream
With the man who'd played with Anson on the old
  Chicago team.

It made our eyeballs nigh pop out and pop back in again
To hear that Casey tellin' of old Anson and his men;
Why home runs wuz so common that nobody waved a
  hat,
With Williamson,[4] King Kelly,[5] or Fred Pfeffer [6] at the
  bat;

Cap Anson, on whose old Chicago team the
Casey, in one of Grantland Rice's ballads,
is said to have been the bat boy.

A man who didn't hit above .500 couldn't stick
With that old bunch, for Anson would release him mighty
quick;
They handled ground balls with their teeth and often
shut their eyes
While in the act of pullin' down the longest, hardest flies;
And after all the "fannin' bees" [7] each night we used to
dream
Of the man who played with Anson on the old Chicago
team.

But somehow this feller Casey never felt like goin' in;
He spent his time at Wilson's shakin' poker dice [8] for
gin.
Whenever he wuz needed he wuz always sure to shirk,
Remarkin' he would have to wait before he started work.
If any other gent had loafed the way he used to do,
We'd have fined him fifty dollars every day, and benched
him too;
But you see the fans respected him and backed him to the
last
On account of his connections with the diamond in the
past,
For no one felt like knockin' or handin' out a call
To the man who'd played on Anson's team, the greatest
of 'em all.

Wal, finally the climax came—the big test of the year—
And the fans wuz there in bunches from the country far
and near,
Especially attracted by the statement made that day
That, having rounded into shape, big Casey wuz to play.
The other nine wuz lookin' kinder worried and upset,
And they wouldn't even listen to an even-money bet.
We kidded 'em and joshed 'em, but no wagerin' wuz
done,
Till at last they placed a thousand at the odds of ten
to one;
But even at these odds it looked an easy-money scheme,
With the man who'd played with Anson on the old
Chicago team.

But Casey never drew a chance to shine in any way;
They handed him a base on balls without the least delay;

57

The pitcher didn't seem to care to put one over straight
While the man who'd played with Anson was a-standin'
at the plate.
He only had one fly in left, which bounded off his head
(It seems the sun was shinin' in his countenance, he said);
And so the people waited in much anger and suspense
For Casey's opportunity to drive one through the fence;
And it came—O yes—it landed with a nauseating rap
For the man who'd played with Anson, and referred to
him as "Cap."

Old Mudville was a run behind when that last inning
came;
The bases full and two wuz out—a hit would win the
game.
"He's got to put it over now," each rooter waved his hat,
And shouted in delirium as Casey stepped to bat.
The first two inshoots jumped across the center of the
plate,
As Mr. Anson's college chum found out a bit too late;
The next looked good and Casey swung—there came a
mighty crack—
But the noise originated from the spine in Casey's back.
In reaching for that outshoot he had wrenched the spinal
beam
Of the man who played with Anson on the old Chicago
team.

That night we wired Anson to discover if he knew
A man by name of Casey, as we felt we ought to do;
And when the answer came next day it stirred up quite a
fuss:
"Yes, I remember Casey well—he carried bats for us."

We hunted for him quite a spell, but he had gone away,
Else the daisies would be bloomin' over his remains
to-day.
But if you land in Mudville on the lookout for some fun,
Don't ever mention Casey's name unless you wear a gun.

8. HE NEVER HEARD OF CASEY!

by Grantland Rice

IN 1926, when Rice's column "The Sportlight" appeared daily in the *New York Herald Tribune*, he received the following letter:

Dear Sir:
I have just read your *Casey's Revenge*, which I understand is a sequel to *Casey at the Bat*. I had never heard of this poem before. Where can I get a copy?
L.F.K.

Rice devoted his entire column, on June 1, 1926, page 23, to a poem inspired by this unbelievable query. The poem was reprinted with trivial alterations (some of which may have been printer's errors) on July 1, 1957, three years after Rice's death. What follows is the original version.

HE NEVER HEARD OF CASEY!

I knew a cove [1] who'd never heard of Washington and Lee,
Of Caesar and Napoleon from the ancient jamboree,
But, bli'me, there are queerer things than anything
  like that,
For here's a cove who never heard of "Casey at the Bat"!

He never heard of Mudville and its wild and eerie call,
"When Flynn let drive a single, to the wonderment of all,"
Nor the stormy roar of welcome that "recoiled upon the
  flat,
As Casey, mighty Casey, was advancing to the bat."

"There was ease in Casey's manner," from the Ernest
  Thayer style,
"There was pride in Casey's bearing," and his tanned face
  wore a smile,
And when they thundered "Attaboy!" of course he tipped
  his hat,
But here's a cove who never heard of "Casey at the Bat"!

"Who is Casey?" Can you beat it? Can a thing like this
  be true?
Is there one who's missed the drama that ripped Mudville through and through?
Is there a fan with soul so dead he never felt the sway
Of these famous lines by Thayer in the good old Thayer
  way?

"Ten thousand eyes were on him as he rubbed his hands
  with dirt;
Five thousand tongues applauded as he wiped them on
  his shirt;
Then while the writhing pitcher ground the ball into his
  hip,
Defiance gleamed in Casey's eye, a sneer curled Casey's
  lip."

The drama grew in force and flame, and Berserk went the
  mob,
With Casey representing more than Hornsby, Ruth, or
  Cobb;

Babe Ruth, the closest man in baseball
history to the legendary Casey.

And as the pitcher cut one loose as if fired from a gat—
Say, here's a guy who never heard of "Casey at the Bat"!

"The sneer is gone from Casey's lip, his teeth are clenched
    in hate;
He pounds with cruel violence his bat upon the plate."
And as the pitcher shot one through to meet the final
    test,
There's one low and benighted fan who never heard the
    rest.

Ten million never heard of Keats, or Shelley, Burns, or
    Poe;
But they know "the air was shattered by the force of
    Casey's blow";
They never heard of Shakespeare, nor of Dickens, like
    as not,
But they know the somber drama from old Mudville's
    haunted lot.

He never heard of Casey! Am I dreaming? Is it true?
Is fame but wind-blown ashes when the summer day is
    through?
Does greatness fade so quickly and is grandeur doomed
    to die
That bloomed in early morning, ere the dusk rides down
    the sky?

Is there nothing left immortal in this somber vale called
    Earth?
Is there nothing that's enduring in its guarding shell of
    worth?
Is everything forgotten as the new age stumbles on
And the things that we once cherished make their way to
    helengon?

Is drifting life but dust and dreams to fade within a
    flash,
Where one forgets the drama of the Master and the Ash? [2]
Where one has missed the saga with its misty flow of tears,
Upon that day of tragedy beyond the tramping years?

"Oh! Somewhere in this favored land the sun is shining
    bright;

The band is playing somewhere, and somewhere hearts
  are light;
And somewhere men are laughing, and somewhere children shout,
But there is no joy in Mudville—mighty Casey has struck
  out!"

Rise, De Wolf Hopper, in your wrath, and cut the
  blighter down!
Although Wang [3] may be forgotten in the passing of
  renown,
There's a graver crime committed which should take you
  to the mat,
For here's a cove who never heard of "Casey at the Bat"!

I had an epic written which I thought would never die,
Where they'd build a statue for me with its head against
  the sky;
I said "This will live forever"—but I've canned it in the
  vat,
For here's a guy who never heard of "Casey at the Bat"!

9. CASEY THE COMEBACK

by Herman J. Schiek

Casey the Comeback surely describes the same game that Grantland Rice wrote about in *Casey's Revenge,* even though there are discrepancies between the two accounts. Rice says there were 10,000 fans (twice as many as saw the earlier game in which Casey struck out), Schiek says there were only 5,000, as before. Rice has the score four to one in the last half of the ninth, Schiek has it two to nothing. And when Casey comes to bat there are, according to Rice, three men on base instead of two as in Schiek's version. It seems unlikely that the second game would so closely parallel the earlier one, as it does in Schiek's ballad, but in the absence of better records, it is impossible to say which version is the more accurate.

Casey the Comeback appeared in *Baseball Magazine,* September, 1914, page 79, with the by-line, Herman L. Schiek. A 1924 *Who's Who in America* lists Herman *John* Schiek, a Protestant clergyman who was president of Elmhurst College, in Illinois, from 1919 to 1924. He was, the entry says, a contributor of poems to magazines. Could it be that the editors of *Baseball Magazine* misread the Reverend Schiek's middle initial as L instead of J, or, perhaps, just made a typographical error?

I wrote to Elmhurst College. The public relations office informed me that Dr. Herman J. Schick (the family name had been changed shortly after Dr. Schiek left the university) did indeed write poems. However, in the opinion of another former president and a former faculty member, both at Elmhurst during Dr. Schiek's term of office, it was "extremely doubtful" that he wrote *Casey the Comeback*. "His verses covered subject matter other than baseball," the letter continued, "in which he had no interest whatever."

But college presidents and ministers often have corners of personality that are hidden from their colleagues. I got in touch with Dr. Schiek's son, Armin F. Schick, a medical doctor in Chicago, where his father had been a minister until his death in 1949. Armin Schick has kindly given permission to quote his reply.

My brother and I are unable to document our father's authorship of the poem in question. Intuition, however, makes us confident that he did write it. . . . We have only a small volume of his poems [*Afterwards*, Boston: The Stratford Company, 1931], which does not include *Casey the Comeback*, but does contain *The Prize-fighter* and *The Jockey*.

My father was catcher on his college team and his older brother coached a high school baseball team in St. Louis for a number of years. He was well acquainted with *Casey at the Bat* and my brother recalls that he recited passages from it.

Authorship of a humorous poem was consistent with his outgoing personality. Nor would the distant thunder of 1914 have repressed his exuberance. On one occasion, in the early days of his ministry, he shocked some of his parishioners (our mother's version) by shooting at a passing flight of ducks from the front steps of his country church.

There the matter stands. Perhaps a reader of this book has information that will clinch the matter.

CASEY THE COMEBACK

The Mudville fans were sick and sore for many a summer
day
And through the gloom in Mudville town there shone no
cheering ray,
For the theme of every gossip, the talk in every hall,
Was how the mighty Casey had failed to hit the ball.

And Mudville scorned the mighty man who failed to win
the fray,
They found their golden idol was made of common clay;
They called him every epithet their scorn could conjure
up,
And everybody shunned him from the mayor to the pup.

That same old club came back one day that beat the
Mudville nine,
That same old pitcher graced the slab and smiled a smile
benign.
The Mudville fans looked on aghast, and 'twas with
aching heart,
For Mudville veterans didn't have a look-in ¹ from the
start.

The baseball battle fiercely raged beneath a scorching sun,
And in the last half of the ninth the score stood two to
none;
Then Flynn again hit safely, to the wonderment of all,
And Blake again lambasted the leather from the ball.

Five thousand shouting fans went wild and beat the torrid
air,
Pop bottles showered the ground like rain and gleamed
like diamonds there.
They flashed the message to the town where whistles
screamed like sin,
And e'en the church bells started loose and swelled the
deafening din.

In the coacher's box the manager pranced wildly up and
down,
He challenged nations to a fight, he blessed the good old
town.

He yelled and whistled, pawed the air, and gave the tango
 dance,
And then he stood as petrified—for now was Casey's
 chance!

His eye shot toward the mourner's bench, where lonely
 Casey sat,
His cap pulled deep upon his face, his teeth sunk in his
 bat.
He saw the fire in Casey's eye—he saw his look of hate—
And then in accents hoarse and harsh he called him to
 the plate.

And from five thousand throats or more there rose a
 dismal groan.
The faces in the stands went white, the bleachers gave a
 moan—
A moan that had the sadness of the black and awful pit,
For Casey—he who lost that game—was asked to get a hit.

But Casey grimly grabbed his bat and at the plate he
 stood.
The pitcher smiled, the catcher laughed behind his wiry
 hood.
And Casey's face went red with wrath, and then grew
 deadly pale,
For once he knew how feels the dog with a tin can at his
 tail.

The first one over was too wide, but the umpire called it
 "fair."
(He ought to have been flayed alive and roasted then and
 there.)
The second one was far too low, but the umpire yelled
 "Strike tiew."
And round the soul of Casey the air grew strangely blue.

A deathlike stillness gripped the fans, and e'en the groans
 had died;
There were no cheers for Casey now, but only, "Drat his
 hide!"
And again the pitcher loosed the ball, and again—but
 what was that?

It sounded like the crack of doom—but it came from
  Casey's bat!

Ten thousand eyes then saw the ball, as if it had been shot
From out some rifled cannon's mouth—and it traveled
  sizzling hot:
It swirled aloft o'er centerfield into the sky's clear blue—
It rapidly became a speck, then vanished from the view.

And then five thousand throats loosed up and yelled like
  men gone mad!
Ten thousand arms waved furiously, and hats went to the
  bad.
And from the blistering bleachers to the grandstand's
  swellest guy
They wept and laughed and cussed and blessed till all
  their throats went dry.

Oh! Somewhere in our baseball land the shadows thickly
  fall,
The winds are sighing somewhere, and somewhere hangs
  death's pall,
And somewhere hearts are breaking, and towns are reft
  of fame—
But there is no gloom in Mudville, for Casey won the
  game.

10. WHY CASEY WHIFFED

by Don Fairbairn

LIKE so many other baseball greats, Casey was a superstitious fellow who may well have blamed his strike out on the cross-eyed batboy who handed him his bat. It was widely rumored at the time that the boy had been planted in the lot by Fireball Snedeker, the Centerville pitcher, for the express purpose of rattling Casey, but the rumor was never verified. Lee Allen, the well-known historian of baseball, called my attention to this poem by Don Fairbairn, of the *Philadelphia Evening Bulletin*. It appeared in *Sporting News,* January 10, 1937, page 4, column 4. For the real reason for Casey's whiff, see *The Man Who Fanned Casey*.

WHY CASEY WHIFFED [1]

The ball fans always wondered, and in Mudville most
  of all
Why the Mighty Mr. Casey did not clout that final ball,
Did not poke the old potato into stratospheric space,
When the winning runs were rotting there on third and
  second base.

Now a cousin of a neighbor of great Casey's furnace man,
Who was there that eve' when he came home to meet
  the sneering pan
Of his wife, and her six brothers, and a dozen other guys,
Blames the whole thing on a batboy who had bandy-
  legged eyes.

He was never seen before then, and he vanished with the
  game,
Like those runts in fairy stories which they tell me did
  the same.
He had red hair and was toothless and he said his name
  was "Buck,"
And his every move and action was a-dripping with bad
  luck.

Casey took the bat he handed, then he felt "all odd" he
  said,
At the plate the awful vision of those optics filled his
  head.
Sure, they whiffed [1] him, but he realized as the fans
  groaned to the skies,
He was hoo-dooed [2] by the urchin with the double-cross-
  ing eyes!

11. CASEY AT THE PLATE

W. B. France

IN THE many poems that have been written about Casey, little has been said of one of his most admirable character traits: his unimpeachable honesty. The following ballad tells of a second unhappy occasion on which Mudville, thanks this time to Casey's inability to tell a lie, also lost the game.

I found this poem in *Aunt Minnie's Scrapbook: Humorous Tales of the Diamond*, by Albert Kennedy ("Rosey") Roswell, an undated booklet of seventy-nine pages published by the Fort Pitt Brewing Company, in Pittsburgh. No author was credited. After my book was published, Lydon E. Amy sent me a copy of the ballad he had clipped from a magazine, probably in the 1930s, but he could not recall the magazine's name. The poem had the byline of W. B. France, about whom I know nothing.

CASEY AT THE PLATE

The Mudville hopes for victory were fading mighty fast;
The team was trailing nine to eight, the inning was the
   last.
And from the friendly bleacher bunch, there rose a vocal
   din;
"Don't worry, Boys! The game's the thing, and may the
   best team win!"

The Mudville catcher came to bat, they fanned him, one,
   two, three.
The second baseman popped a fly, the second out was he.
And then the crowd began to cheer—stupendous, hopeful,
   great.
For Casey, Honest Casey, was advancing to the plate!

The pitcher threw, and Casey swung; he hit the empty
   air.
Another pitch and Casey made his strikes an even pair.
And then a lusty bleacher voice, a helpful thought
   advanced:
"Go get the guy a snowshoe! Let him have a sportin'
   chance!"

The managers conferred and soon the fact was brought to
   light
That each believed, "The customer is always in the
   right."
So Casey got a snowshoe and he slammed a hefty swat
That sent the ball a sailin' to the corner of the lot!

The fielder ran to get the ball as Casey rounded first;
He picked it up as Casey got to second with a burst
Of speed that took him on to third before the ball was
   tossed,
So Casey speeded down to home without a second lost.

Casey, ball and catcher came together at the plate,
And hope for Mudville dangled in the fickle hands of fate.
A hush descended on the fans who waited for the ump [1]
To let them know if Casey was a hero or a chump.

All eyes were turned on Casey as the umpire scratched his
   head.

"I do believe in being frank and truthful, boys," he said.
The play was close, I couldn't get a clear and ample view,
So to back a fair decision, I'll leave it up to you."

Oh; somewhere people brood about decadence of man-
kind,
They moan that truth and probity are mighty hard to
find;
But Mudville hails an honest man whose heart is true and
stout,
For Casey said: "I cannot lie. He tug me, boys, I'm out!"

12. THE COMING BACK OF CASEY

by Charles E. Jestings

THERE are two known later occasions on which Casey, coming to bat at a climactic moment in the ninth inning, faced his old enemy, Fireball Snedeker. On both occasions Casey's bat connected with the ball. The following ballad by Charles E. Jestings (does any reader know who he might be?) appeared in *Baseball Magazine,* May, 1937, p. 544, and tells the story of one of those occasions. Whether it took place before or after that glorious swat first described by Grantland Rice, and later by Herman J. Schiek, has not yet been determined.

THE COMING BACK OF CASEY

A brilliant star was Casey out on Mudville's famous flat;
A ball-hawk in the field was he, a marvel at the bat;
His name was sought for autographs, his portrait for
 the wall—
Indeed, immortal Casey was the wizard of them all!

But even so, all Mudville tasted rank defeat that day
When Casey, like a Brodie,[1] let the pennant slip away—
A slim, ungainly hurler came advancing on the town,
And, working nicely in the pinch, set Mighty Casey down.

As Casey went out swinging, not a soul could shriek or
 shout.
The audience was petrified when Casey had struck out.
They couldn't feel, or hear or hope, but only see and
 sigh,
And fain believe this tragedy some black magician's lie.

Their thought to wreck the grandstand wasn't easy to
 resist—
There had so much depended on the ball Great Casey
 missed!
The thing stuck in the nimble mind of every rabid fan—
So everywhere that Casey went, they put him on the pan!

"A tennis racket, Casey!" "Strike out!" "Hit it with a
 board!"
The pack of wolves were on him now, a wild, abusive
 horde.
They rode him when he stepped to bat or gathered in a
 fly,
But Casey's only answer was the challenge in his eye.

One editor suggested to the club's aristocrats
A trade involving Casey for a pair of real good bats,
And added, sort of slyly, that in case a deal went through,
There'd be no crime committed, nor could anybody sue!

From such humiliation would a timid novice fly;
'Twould cause bold veterans to cringe, or craven souls to
 die;
But calm, courageous Casey simply seemed to thrive on it,
And so the louder fandom razzed, the harder Casey hit.

As Casey's big bat echoed, one by one great records fell.
His specialty was homers, and the real old-timers tell
That when great Casey singled, he would streak to first
    and scowl,
As if to say, "That kind of hit's no better than a foul!"

Most frequently long homers did his brutal bludgeon
    pound,
As oft with devastated dreams, sad twirlers left the
    mound;
For Casey smashed them on the nose, he hit them low
    and high
To settle down behind the wall or fade out in the sky.

Thus matters stood when Casey, in the spotlight of re-
    nown,
Faced once again the pitcher who before had set him
    down.
The Mudcats trailed by five to three in inning number
    nine,
With opposing factions deadlocked and the pennant on
    the line.

Yet Mudville's hopes most certainly were not forlorn at
    worst—
McCann had doubled, and when Cole beat out a bunt to
    first[2]
With one away,[3] the goose hung high [4] and ready for the
    crate,[5]
For Casey with his mighty bat was stepping to the plate!

There was art in every action, as he proudly took his
    stance.
That he meant to deal destruction was apparent at a
    glance.
And, when replying to applause, he waved up to the
    crowd
The rousing roar that cheered him would have made a
    monarch proud.

But Casey didn't seem to hear; his keen and anxious eye
Glared at the gangling pitcher his most withering defy;

He dug his cleats into the turf like one who understands
Just how to settle briefly big business on his hands.

The hurler looked him over, coiled himself into a knot,
Then straightening, released the pellet forward like a
    shot!
Hard by the batter's waistline the fiery curve-ball shied.
"Too close for me!" said Casey. "Strike one!" the umpire
    cried.

The multitude, surprised, enraged, sent up a vicious
    groan
Like a den of roaring lions bent on tearing flesh from
    bone—
The ump had called a rank one, but they couldn't rub
    him out—
They saw that far too many cops with billies stood about.

This robbery Great Casey did not protest or resist—
He took it smiling broadly like a big philanthropist;
With quiet ease of manner and with spirit unperplexed,
He stood as if announcing, "I am ready for the next!"

The gawky moundsman faced again his foeman from the
    hill.
No movement stirred the quiet air. The crowd grew
    very still.
And there in calm assurance and in patience all could
    feel,
Great Casey stood with waving bat and nerve as stout as
    steel.

The twirler gripped the ball; he paused; an instant held
    it high.
Then suddenly his arm came down and let it homeward
    fly!
There was a sharp, resounding smack that rang from wall
    to wall,
The sound a solid bludgeon makes when laid against a
    ball!

Throughout great cities there was joy and factory
    whistles blew.

And village bells rang lustily with life a brighter hue.
And somewhere there was singing and 'most everywhere
   delight,
Because for someone, somewhere, almost everything went
   right!

And there was joy in Mudville, too! It was a jolly town!
It had its share of laughter. It basked in fine renown.
But *that* was, oh, *so* long ago! It was before that day
When Casey, Mighty Casey, hit into a double play!

13. THE MAN WHO FANNED CASEY

by "Sparkus"

The Man Who Fanned Casey made its first appearance, so far as I have been able to determine, on the other side of one of De Wolf Hopper's recordings of *Casey* (see Note 5, *There Was Ease in Casey's Manner . . .*). The record label gives only the single name "Sparkus" as the ballad's author, and I have been unable to find out who this was or when the ballad was written. The poem—a retelling of the story of Casey's strike out by a Mudville fan unable to conceal his admiration for Fireball Snedeker—supplies many previously unknown details about Snedeker's sneaky strategy.

The Centerville pitcher is called Hagen in Digby Bell's recitation, but this is clearly a mistake. I have changed the name to Fireball, since "Snedeker" has too many syllables to fit the meter, and this was before Snedeker changed his last name to Riley (see *Riley in the Box*). I have also taken the liberty of rewriting a few of the worst lines, including the penultimate one to which I have added a reference to Thatcher, the Centerville catcher. The poem, as I revised it, was reprinted by Tom Seaver in his book, *How I Would Pitch to Babe Ruth* (Playboy Press, 1974).

THE MAN WHO FANNED CASEY

I'm just an ordinary fan, and I don't count for much,
But I'm for writing history with a true and honest touch.
It isn't often that I knock—I'll put you next to that—
But I must interpose a word on *Casey at the Bat.*

Oh, yes, I must admit it; the poem is a beaut.
Been runnin' through my thinker since our team got on
    the chute.[1]
I heard an actor fan recite it thirteen years ago;[2]
He sort of introduced it in the progress of the show.

It made a hit from gallery, down to the parquet floor; [3]
But now I've got to thinking, and that poem makes me
    sore.
I'd like to know why any fan should be so off his nut
About the Mighty Casey who proved himself a mutt.[4]

The score, we're told, stood four to two, one inning left
    to play.
The Frogtown [5] twirler thought he had things pretty
    much his way,
So in the ninth, with two men down, he loosened up a
    bit;
And Flynn scratched out a single, Blake let loose a two-
    base hit.

Then from the stand and bleachers there arose a mighty
    roar.
They wanted just that little hit they knew would tie the
    score.
And there at bat was Casey, Mighty Casey, Mudville's
    pride;
But was the Frogtown slabster [6] sent balloonin',[7] terrified?

Now in the ninth, with two men down and Casey at the
    bat,
Most pitchers would have let him walk—we all are sure of
    that.
But Fireball was a hero, he was made of sterner stuff;
It's *his* kind get the medals and the long newspaper puff.[8]

He knew the time had come for him to play a winning
role.
He heard the fans a-yelling; it was music to his soul.
He saw the gleam of confidence in Mighty Casey's eye.
"I'll strike him out!" Fireball resolved. "I'll do it or I'll
die!"

He stood alone and friendless in that wild and frenzied
throng.
There wasn't even one kind word to boost his game along.
But back in Frogtown where they got the plays by special
wire
The fans stood ready, if he won, to set the town on fire.

Now Fireball twirls his body on the truest corkscrew
plan
And hurls a swift inshoot [9] that cuts the corner of the
pan.[10]
But Casey thought the first ball pitched would surely be a
ball,
And didn't try to strike it, to the great disgust of all.

Again the Frogtown twirler figures dope on Mudville's
pride; [11]
And Casey thinks the next will be an outshoot breaking
wide.[12]
But Fireball shot a straight one down the middle of the
plate,
And Casey waited for a curve until it was too late.

A now the mighty slugger is a-hangin' on the string.[13]
If another good one comes along, it's up to him to swing.
The jaunty smile, Fireball observed, has faded from his
face,
And a look of straining agony is there to take its place.

One moment Fireball pauses, hides the ball behind his
glove,
And then he drives it from him with a sweeping long arm
shove.
And now the air is shattered, and the ball's in Thatcher's
mitt,
For Casey, Mighty Casey, hadn't figured on the spit! [14]

14. CASEY ON A BAT

by William F. Kirk

THIS short poem by William Frederick Kirk first appeared in the *New York Evening Journal* and was later included in Kirk's small book of baseball ballads, *Right off the Bat* (G. W. Dillingham, 1911). The poetry isn't much, but the pun deserves a chuckle. There also exists a much longer and more libelous ballad called *Casey and the Bat* [1] (the word "bat" is here a term for prostitute) that I found in a friend's mimeographed collection of pornography, *Lost Limericks and Bar Room Ballads,* no compiler, no date. (Don't write to ask for a copy; all such inquiries will remain unanswered.) Kirk's Casey, one must note, is on the Boston team and should not be confused with Mudville's Casey.

Casey and the Bat, illustrated by Blair Gibeau, was privately published in 1988 by the Polo Grounds Press, in Cincinnati. It is now a rare collector's item.

CASEY ON A BAT

It looked extremely rocky for the Boston team that day,
The score was one to nothing, with one inning left to
play.
Casey, who played center field, had shown one hour too
late—
He hadn't any alibi when staggering through the gate.
So when he tore his necktie off and stepped upon his hat
The manager looked grim and said, "It's Casey on a bat."

"Well," said the Boston manager, "with joy I ought to
scream—
Here's Casey with a dandy load, the best man on the
team.
He told me he was sober, but he couldn't quite get by
When he stepped upon his derby and was yanking off his
tie.
Of all the hard luck in the world! The mean, ungrateful
rat!
A blooming championship at stake and Casey on a bat."

Two Boston batters in the ninth were speedily retired,
"Here, Casey!" cried the manager, speaking as one in-
spired,
"Go in and bat for Grogan! There's a man on second
base,
And if you hit the way you can we'll win the pennant
race."
This is no knock on buttermilk, or anything like that,
But the winning hit was made that day by Casey on a bat.

15. MRS. CASEY AT THE BAT

Author unknown

CENTERVILLE is a small town on the western border of Linn County, Kansas, about seven miles east of where Mudville once stood. In the 1890's it was a company town dominated by Post's Nut and Bolt Manufacturing Company. The following ballad recalls an occasion in 1893 on which the Mudville girls' softball team played the Boltsy-Nutsy Frails on their home ground. The poem appears without a by-line in *Aunt Minnie's Scrapbook* (see the introduction to *Casey at the Plate*), and I have been unable to trace it to its source.

MRS. CASEY AT THE BAT

'Twas the day of the great big softball game with the
    Boltsy-Nutsy Frails,
The score stood eighteen-twenty and six broken finger-
    nails;
And when Betty [1] turned her ankle and Ethel [2] burst a
    seam,
The fans were so disgusted they were almost fit to scream.

A straggling few got up to go and get a malted milk,
The rest swapped recipes or showed each other bits of
    silk;
For they felt the girls had let them down particularly
    flat
Unless—and quite unlikely—Nellie Casey [3] got to bat.

Dot Flynn [4] preceded Nellie, to say nothing of Mae Breen,
And the less you said the better, if you know just what I
    mean—
Though don't ever say I said it—they were both of them
    too fat.
There was little chance of Mrs. Casey getting to the bat.

But Flynnsie shut her eyes and swung (it almost killed
    them all)
And Maisie did a rhumba which connected with the ball,
And when the dust had lifted—well I'll be a dirty word—
There was Maisie Breen on second, and Dot Flynn was
    safe on third.

Then the stands reverberated with soprano shrieks of glee,
Their wads of gum they swallowed when the fans thought
    what they'd see;
And two girls kissed each other (though each thought
    each a cat)
For Mrs. Nellie Casey was advancing to the bat.

How they clapped for Mrs. Casey as she stepped into her
    place,
Her corset fitted perfectly, she moved about with grace;
This was her chosen universe of which she was the hub,
(While back in their apartment, Casey waited for his
    grub).

"Well, throw the ball, Estelle," she cried, "and get it over, do!"
And blushing with self-consciousness, the Boltsy pitcher threw.
"By me," said Mrs. Casey, in her best bridge-player's voice,
"It's much too low!" But just the same, "Strike!" was the umpire's choice.

"You nasty man!" The girls went wild, in accents loud and shrill,
"You brute! You boor! You peasant! You idiot! You pill!"
"Oh, kill him! Kill him!" were the cries that rose from out the stand.
They'd have beaned him with their compacts had not Nell held up her hand.

With savoir-faire that would have drawn a nod from Mrs. Post,[5]
She signaled for the second pitch and stilled the angry host;
"Come on, Estelle, try hard, dear, do—you know the kind I like—"
Again the ball came over and again the ump cried "Strike!"

"Boo!" screamed the crowd. The catcher grinned, "It's raw, but don't you mind,
The shine from off your nose, my dear, has drove the umpire blind."
That's all that Mrs. Casey heard. That's all, but 'twas enough,
A shiny nose—five thousand fans—and where's her powder puff?

The Casey smile is set and grim; no longer does she speak.
Her thoughts are in the Powder Room, and on that gleaming beak.
And now the pitcher holds the ball, and now she lets it go,
And now the air is shattered with Mrs. Casey's blow.

Oh, somewhere in this favored land good husbands get a
    break,
Somewhere they feast on crisp french fries and tender,
    juicy steak;
But a girl can't bat with a shiny nose, of that there is no
    doubt,
So Casey eats cold beans tonight—Mrs. Casey has struck
    out!

16. CASEY'S SON

by Nitram Rendrag

CASEY's oldest son, Angus Barry (born 1888), grew up to be a ball player for a short period during his late teens. The story of an embarrassing occasion in August, 1905, when (like his father eighteen years earlier) he was responsible for the loss of an important game, is told by Nitram Rendrag in the following ballad. It is here published for the first time.

CASEY'S SON

The Story of a Terrible Downfall

The game had almost ended. The sun was hanging low.
Slamtown [1] was leading six to three, one inning yet to go.
Two outs for Mudville, none on base, with Dibble [2] at
    the plate;
And Dibble's batting average was the lowest in the state.

But Dibble drove a double, much to everyone's surprise,
And when Pringle [3] binged a bingle, [4] you should have
    heard the cries!
With Dibs on third and Pring on first, the hopes of
    Mudville rose,
For the son of Mighty Casey was advancing on his toes.

Yes, the son of Mighty Casey tiptoed carefully to his
    place.
There was caution in his bearing and a frown upon his
    face.
In the dugout he'd been guzzling beer and never
    dreaming that
He'd have the opportunity of getting up to bat.

Young Casey was a trifle plump, but had a lot of guts.
The fans all called him "Butterball" or sometimes just
    plain "Butts."
His height: five feet, five inches. His weight: two hundred
    pounds.
His habit: whacking balls beyond the borders of the
    grounds.

Young Casey burped and swung and missed. A rooter
    bellowed "Boo!"
He swung and missed and burped again. The ump called
    out "Strike two!"
The third was high, the fourth was low, the fifth pitch
    grazed his cheek.
Casey hitched his beltless pants. He gave his cap a tweak.

The pitcher winds. He cuts it loose. Young Casey shuts
    his eyes.

He swings a monstrous swing and—crack!—the pill is in
the skies!
Dibble dances home while Pring is prancing on to third
And Casey's rounding first. The ball's still winging like
a bird.

The men in left and center fields are racing toward the
sphere.
When Pringle trots across home plate, the fans jump up
and cheer.
"I've got it!" shouts one fielder. The other yells "She's
mine!"
They bump. They fall. The baseball smacks an advertising sign.

It bounces back. One man gets up, retrieves it, throws it,
stumbling;
While Casey gallops on to home, perspiring, stomach
rumbling.
A mighty burp! Two buttons pop. His legs are tied in
knots.
His trousers hang below his knees! His shorts have polka
dots!

Poor Casey's face is cherry red. He trips and almost falls.
He tries to pull his trousers up. Alas, too late, the ball's
Now nestled in the catcher's mitt. Young Casey spins and
snorts.
He heads for third but feels the pill that's pressed against
his shorts.

Somewhere, tonight, in Kansas, there are happy men
and boys
Who are celebrating victory and making lots of noise.
There is singing, dancing, laughing, but it's in another
town.
There is only gloom in Mudville since poor Casey's pants
fell down.

17. CASEY'S SISTER AT THE BAT

by James O'Dea

JAMES O'Dea, who wrote the following ballad about Casey's younger sister, Hortense, came to the United States about 1903 from Hamilton, Ontario. He married Anne Caldwell, a playwright; the two collaborated on the lyrics of some new songs for *The Wizard of Oz*, a musical then enjoying a sensational run since its opening in 1902. O'Dea wrote other popular songs of the time, and collaborated on several musical comedies. He died in 1914 at the age of forty-three, at his home in Rockville Centre, Long Island, N.Y. *Jingleman Jack*, a small book of his verse, was published in New York by Saalfield Publishing Co., in 1901. His earlier book, *Daddy Long Legs' Fun Songs*, was published by Whitmark in 1900, with illustrations and format similar to L. Frank Baum's first successful book, *Father Goose*. The Christmas 1969 issue of *The Baum Bugle* (official organ of the International Wizard of Oz Club) provides details about the three songs that O'Dea wrote for *The Wizard* musical.

Casey's Sister at the Bat is my own title for his ballad which originally appeared as *Casey the Second* in *Baseball Magazine*, February, 1911, page 71. O'Dea never explains Hortense's exact relation to Casey, but my research into Mudville history has disclosed that Casey did have a sister named Hortense. I have altered O'Dea's last line (originally: "Of Casey the Second who failed at the bat.") to make this clear, and have also placed quotation marks around "varsity," in the third stanza, to avoid another bit of ambiguity.

CASEY'S SISTER AT THE BAT

What! You missed the big game, and you'd have me tell
Your friend of the manner in which we fell
To the Vassar eight with our speed reversed?
I will—If you introduce me first.

Charmed! I assure you—Why surely, indeed,
We play only eight on a side—Agreed,
For the sun-field can freckle till one is incensed,
So, with that position [1] we girls have dispensed.

Well, the Vassar Delights [2]—all lovely girls, too,
Came up from their "varsity" bringing a crew
Of rooters and fans whose desire, it would seem,
Was to jump on the necks of our lady-like team.

And all through the game they were dreadfully rude,
My dear, it was shameful as fiercely they boo'ed
And shouted, "Oh, sweet!" and "Why don't you slide!"
With a lot more unheeded advice on the side.

The game as a contest was perfectly cute
Except for the umpire, and he was a brute:
From the talk that went 'round I should judge the old
   dunce
Was a robber, a blockhead and fool all at once.

For eight hands around—Yes, innings, I mean,
'Twas the darlingest thing of the kind I have seen.
Twenty-three—twenty-three [3] was the score on the fence—
Precisely—a tie—with excitement intense.

When the Vassars got through with their stunt at the bat
In the ninth and last innings I thought it was "scat!"
For the girls of our side, for when finished, they had
Five runs to the good which, of course, made it bad.

But we didn't care though the going seemed rough,
Not one of our crowd even wilted a puff
Till two of our team were put out—so were we—
Wanting two extra runs if the winners we'd be.

"But wait!" said a girl at my side who was "wise,"
"Just wait till we hand 'em the gentle surprise.
Are we there with a something concealed up our sleeve?
Just rub up your glasses and see, and believe!

"Ah! here she is now! Can you beat her for class!
Will she get the runs? Will a rabbit eat grass!
'Who is she?' Why, Casey—Hortense Casey who
Can lace that old ball as she'd lace her own shoe."

With two on the bases and fire in her eyes
To the plate she advances and somebody cries:
"Now, Casey, come on, put it over the fence."
"You bet you, I will," said the smiling Hortense.

And then it began—Well, I'd rather not say
What was said to the umpire that memorable day
As there he stood calling, "Strike One!" and "Strike
    Two!"—
All umpires are horrid, I think so, don't you?

"And now," said the girl who was wise, "this is It—
That pitcher is there with a pretty good 'spit,'
But watch dear old Casey cut loose with a swat
That will land it beyond the confines of the lot."

The ball comes to Casey, who swings with her bat,
And fiercely she strikes—where the ball isn't at—
The catcher has caught it—complete is the rout
With "His Umps" saying: "Sister, that's three and you're
    out!"

And that's how we happened to lose the big game,
There was nothing momentous about it, I claim,
Except for the tale that it furnishes—that
Of Casey's kid sister who failed at the bat.

18. CASEY'S DAUGHTER
AT THE BAT

by Al Graham

AL Graham's delightful account of a 1906 game between the girls' softball teams of Mudville and Centerville first appeared in Franklin P. Adams's column, "The Conning Tower," *New York Post*, June 29, 1939. It is reprinted here from F.P.A.'s anthology, *Innocent Merriment* (McGraw-Hill, 1942, page 490) with the permission of the author, the publisher, and Mrs. Adams. Al Graham, who has written several books of verse for children, now lives in Oradell, New Jersey. Patsy Casey (born 1889) was seventeen when the events of the poem took place.

CASEY'S DAUGHTER AT THE BAT

The outlook wasn't brilliant for the Mudvillettes, it
    seems;
The score stood four to two against that best of softball
    teams;
And when Brenda ("Lefty") Cooney [1] and "Babs" Bar-
    rows [2] both flied out,
A sickly silence filled the air, and the fans began to pout.

A straggling few got up to go—'twas the ninth and two
    were down—
While the rest had little hope at all that the 'Ettes would
    Go To Town;
Still, they thought if only Casey's gal—Patricia—Patsy—
    Pat—
Could get a lick, they still might win with Casey at the
    bat.

But Myrna Flynn [3] and Hedy Blake [4] had to hit before
    Miss C.;
And the former was a sissy, and the latter just a she;
So again upon a Mudville throng grim melancholy sat,
For there seemed no chance whatever that Patricia'd get
    to bat.

But Myrna smacked a single, to the wonderment of all,
And Hedy—known as Flatfoot—fairly flattened out the
    ball;
And when the dust had lifted, there on third and second
    base
Perched a pair of Mudville cuties, each a-powdering her
    face.

Then from the howling mamas in the stand in back of
    first
Went up a weird, unearthly scream, like a Tarzan crazed
    with thirst,
Like a million screeching monkey-fans, like a yowling
    giant cat;
For Casey, Patsy Casey, was advancing to the bat!

There was ease in Patsy's manner as she stepped up to the
  plate;
There were curves in Patsy's figure, and a bounce in
  Patsy's gait;
And when responding to the screams she lightly doffed
  her hat,
No Casey fan could doubt 'twas Mighty's daughter at the
  bat.

Ten thousand eyes were on her shorts, an orchidaceous
  hue;
Five thousand tongues commented on her blouse of
  beige-and-blue;
And while the ladies chattered "What a shape!" and
  "What a fit!"
Miss Casey gave her shorts a tug and smoothed her blouse
  a bit.

And now the underhanded pitch came hurtling through
  the air,
But Patsy, like her famous dad, just stood a-smiling there;
And when "Strike one!" the umpire [5] yelled as past that
  softball sped,
"That ain't my style!" is what they say Patricia Casey said.

Again, as in the years a-gone, the crowd set up a roar;
Again, they shouted as they had so many years before,
"Kill him! kill the umpire!"; and as once did Patsy's Pop,
Miss Casey raised a staying hand, and mildly said, "Oh,
  stop!"

And smiling like a lady in a teethy toothpaste ad,
Patricia showed that howling mob she wasn't even mad;
She signaled to the pitcher,[6] who again the ball let fly;
And again like Papa Casey's, Patsy's second strike went by.

Anew, the maddened thousands blamed the strike upon
  the ump;
A racketeer, they labeled him, a floogie,[7] and a frump; [8]
But once again the mob was stilled by Patsy's charming
  smile,
As certain every fan became she'd hit the next a mile.

And now they see her daub a bit of powder on her nose;
They watch her put fresh lipstick on—a shade called Fleur
de Rose;
And now the pitcher holds the ball, and now she lets it go;
And now the air is shattered by *another* Casey's blow.

Oh! somewhere in this favored land the moon is shining
bright;
And somewhere there are softball honeys winning games
tonight.
And somewhere there are softball fans who scream and
yell and shout;
But there's still no joy in Mudville—Casey's *daughter*
has struck out.

19. CASEY'S DREAM

by William F. Robertson

IT IS regrettable that the incident described in the next ballad turns out to be a dream. The thought of Casey pitching in a pinch to his nemesis, Fireball Snedeker, is delicious, and one can see in Casey's dream his strong desire to clobber Fireball, one way or another. The poem bore the by-line of William F. Robertson when it appeared in *Baseball Magazine,* January, 1936, page 364. I have been unable to learn anything about the author.

CASEY'S DREAM

As the dismal shades of evening gathered in his lonely
room,
All alone sat mighty Casey, staring at the murky gloom,
And the smile that once was Casey's now was covered with
a frown,
For his crime had brought dishonor he could never quite
live down.

So his head was bowed in sorrow, as he wondered just why
Fate
Had so painfully restrained him as he stood there at the
plate;
In his ears there still was ringing every tantalizing shout,
And he still could hear them telling how that pitcher
struck him out.

As he sat there in the twilight wondering just what he'd
do,
Asking if his shameful failure meant his baseball days
were through,
Deep fatigue began to challenge and his strength began to
creep,
Then his weary eyelids yielded, and poor Casey fell asleep.

Once again he heard the plaudits as he raced back to the
wall
And pulled down a mighty liner,[1] to the wonderment of
all,
And their words fell on his eardrums like a mother's
lullaby,
And he told himself in secret he'd avenge himself or die.

Things looked bright for dear old Mudville, thanks to
Casey's potent mace,
And that look of grim defiance crept again o'er Casey's
face,
For he felt that his great comeback was another task well
done,
And he knew he'd live forever in the hearts of everyone.

But the final inning started, as those last ones sometimes
do,
And the pitching staff of Mudville seemed to suddenly fall
through;
All were tried and all resembled water running from a
ditch,
"Mr. Manager," said Casey, "let me go in there and
pitch."

Arrogance again ruled Casey as he stepped into the box,
And again he was the captain of a ship upon the rocks;
But his heart leaped up with rapture as he proudly
glanced about,
And discovered that the batter was the man who'd struck
him out.

In the twinkling eyes of Casey confidence gleamed forth
anew;
What a time and situation; what a spot to step into!
Two men out, the score all even, three men resting on the
sacks,
And the promise from the pitcher that he'd stop 'em in
their tracks.

Casey fell into his wind-up like a haughty, handsome
prince,
And the ball went with a swiftness never seen before or
since;
Momentarily they saw it, like the lightning in the night,
But they heard the sound of something stopping leather
in its flight.

Just a foul, that's all, thought Casey, as again he looked
around,
Then he stopped, and shrank with horror, for he saw
there on the ground
Someone lying prone and helpless, resting on his earthly
bed,
For the batter hadn't fouled it, but had stopped it with
his head!

Oh the hand of fate cares little for the lowly or the great,
And the man on third had started and had dashed across
the plate,

And the gallant sons of Mudville once again were put to
  rout,
And the cry went to the heavens, "Mighty Casey knocked
  him out!"

Then a gentle word of comfort fell again on Casey's ear.
"You have been asleep," said someone.[2] "Why you must
  be weary, dear."
"Yes, I'm very tired," said Casey. "Oh this headache is a
  curse.
Could you give me something for it? I believe it's getting
  worse."

20. RILEY IN THE BOX

Author unknown

It is easy to understand how James Riley ("Fireball") Snedeker, the Centerville pitcher who fanned Casey, must have felt in later years. His name is not even mentioned in Thayer's account of the game. Indeed, public resentment against him became so intense that in 1891, when he left Centerville to pitch for the Boston Beaneaters, he changed his last name from Snedeker to Riley, his middle name and the maiden name of his mother. Of course, bands never did serenade him as (in the following sad little ballad) he imagines they should have done. His pitching, though competent, was never great. After retiring from professional baseball in 1908 he returned to Centerville where he opened Riley's Saloon and in 1910 married Hedy Blake, daughter of James Blake, former Mudville third baseman (see Note 4 of *Casey's Daughter at the Bat*).

No author was given for *Riley in the Box* when it appeared in *Aunt Minnie's Scrapbook* (see the introduction to *Casey at the Plate*). I would be pleased to hear from any reader who may know the author of this poem and where it was first published.

RILEY IN THE BOX

There's been a lot of smoking over Casey and his bat,
And how he didn't win the game and other guff like that;
They've made some rhymes about him and that sort of
swelled his fame,
But what's the good of crackin' up [1] the mutt [2] that lost
the game?

I'd heard about this Casey and the way he smashed 'em
out.
I'd heard about his posing just to hear the bleachers
shout.
So when we tackled Casey's team you may be sure I tried
To put a kink in Casey's game and puncture Casey's
pride.

For those of you who seen the game it's easy to recall
That we'd have lost and they'd have won had Casey hit
the ball.
'Twas in the ninth with bases full that Casey came to bat,
And Lordy, how the bleachers cheered when on his hands
he spat.

I doubled up and then unkinked and let the horsehide
fly,
But Casey only stood and smiled and watched the ball
go by.
"One strike!" the umpire shouted, and I thought there'd
be a fight,
But Casey sort of turned and said, "Be quiet, lads, he's
right."

Again I shot a screamer, and it whistled o'er the plate.
If Casey thought he'd strike at it, he thought a bit too late.
"Two strikes!" the umpire bellowed, but the bleachers
didn't shout;
I looked at Casey and I saw his smile was dying out.

I braced myself and sent him one in my peecoolyer style,
And Casey swang with all his might—and missed it by a
mile!

No matter what the po-try says of Casey and his bat,
This is the way it happened, you can lay your coin on
     that.

The bands are playing somewhere, but 'tis not in Casey's
     town;
They're serenading Riley, he's the man who put him
     down.
And "no skiddoo" for Casey's fame, his number's "twenty-
     three!" [3]
'Twas Riley, Pitcher Riley, was the hero, don't you see?

21. CASEY ON THE MOUND

by Harry E. Jones

ALTHOUGH Casey could not tell a lie (see *Casey at the Plate*), he was not above using a bit of deception in the pinches. The following incident calls to mind the antics of that other great Irish batsman, King Kelly. It must have occurred many years after Casey's famous whiff because throughout the ballad Casey is referred to as "old Casey." Note that Thatcher is still catching for Centerville, but Fireball Snedeker has presumably gone to Boston (see *Riley in the Box*). The poem appeared in *Baseball Magazine*, November–December, 1954, page 16, with the by-line of Harry E. Jones. Here and there I have tinkered slightly with original lines.

CASEY ON THE MOUND

It happened in the Bush League, not many years ago—
This little baseball incident, I think you ought to know.
Call it robbery or strategy, or any other name,
It meant a lot to Mudville, for Mudville won the game.

'Twas a warm day in September, in the final play-off
  game,
The Mudville boys were fighting, to gain the Hall of
  Fame.
For fifteen torrid innings they really gave their best,
The boys had played their hearts out, to win the final test.

Then came the sixteenth inning, when things began to
  hum.
On three successive singles Old Mudville scored a run.
That little run looked mighty big. They eyed the board
  with pride.
They knew that all they had to do was hold the other side.

The shades of night were falling when the boys took to
  the field,
To do or die for Mudville; a score they must not yield.
The shades of night were falling as old Casey looked
  around.
The fans were filled with confidence, with Casey on the
  mound.

The first man up for Centerville was put out on a fly.
Casey smiled serenely at the cheer that rent the sky.
The next man went down swinging. Two down, and one
  to go.
The fans were begging Casey: "Make it three men in a
  row."

Then things began to happen, no one knows the reason
  why.
But it seems those pesky visitors had found their batting
  eye.
The next man up there singled; Casey kept him close to
  first,
But his pitching arm was aching, and old Casey feared
  the worst.

He was their only pitcher—they had used up all the rest
In those fifteen torrid innings—so he vowed to do his best.
He threw his favorite sinker, but Thatcher smacked the
   ball,
And the heart went out of Casey as he saw it hit the wall.

He was working very carefully now; the cheering throng
   was stilled.
But Casey walked the next man, so the bases then were
   filled.
With Slugger Bingo [1] coming up, a trifle old but still
A bearcat [2] in the pinches; this boy could swat the pill.

With Casey really bearing down, the count was three and
   two.
A hit now meant the ball game, how well old Casey knew!
He looked out at his fielders, he gazed up at the sky,
He had a grin upon his lips, the devil in his eye.

He signaled to the catcher, and then strolled toward the
   plate.
They met there on the pathway, strategic plans to make.
"It's getting dark," said Casey, "and difficult to see.
If we're to win this ball game, I think it's up to me."

"So I'll go through the motions of throwing you the ball.
Yes, I'll go through the motions, but without a ball at all!
You act as though you make the catch. I'll wait 'til you're
   all set.
It's going to take this strategy to win this ball game yet."

Then Casey walked back to the mound and dusted off
   his hand.
He peered in at the catcher with a manner that was
   grand.
He took his finest wind up, though he felt so queer inside,
Then whipped his arm and let 'er go. "Strike three!" the
   umpire [3] cried.

Old Slugger Bingo, white with rage, pounded on the plate.
The things that he was muttering are too raw to relate.
But when he'd cooled enough to speak, he grabbed the
   ump and cried,
"You blind old bat, you know that ball was a good two
   feet outside!"

22. CASEY—TWENTY YEARS LATER

by Clarence P. McDonald

Casey—Twenty Years Later, which is reprinted in Hazel Felleman's *Best Loved Poems of the American People,* has given me more headaches than any other poem in this book. Miss Felleman credits the ballad to "S. P. McDonald." After exhaustive and futile efforts to find out who this was, or where his poem was first printed (Miss Felleman does not acknowledge a source, and she no longer has her original records), I came upon a poem called *Like Kelly Did,* in *Baseball Magazine* (August, 1916), p. 51, signed "C. P. McDonald." Since this poem, like *Casey—Twenty Years Later,* concerns the Bugville team, there is little doubt that both ballads are by the same man.

I have been unable to determine where *Casey—Twenty Years Later* first appeared, or to obtain any biographical facts about the author. His full name was Clarence Patrick McDonald, and he wrote four small books of inspirational verse of the Eddie Guest, get-up-and-go variety, in praise of American business, advertising, love, sunshine, and things like that. They are: *Cycles* (Cornhill Co., 1918), *Up and Doing* (Carey Craft, 1918), *Songs* (Richardson Press, 1921), and *Step on It!* (Ajax Press, 1925). None contains the two baseball ballads reprinted here.

Casey—Twenty Years Later is second only to *Casey's Revenge* as a sequel that gives Casey a chance to redeem himself. Casey is now forty-eight. The year is 1907. In the last line of the eighth stanza, McDonald refers to him as "short and stocky"; a careless mistake that I have rectified. I have a strong suspicion that some of the ballad's original lines have been garbled. The senseless repetition of "The captain saw his awkward pose" in stanzas 13 and 14 suggests that the original probably had a different phrase in the thirteenth stanza. And the second line of the last stanza fails to meter; a failure easily corrected by substituting a three-syllable adjective, such as "enormous," for "great." I have not tried, however, to rewrite these lines, hoping that some reader of this book can tell me where the ballad first appeared so it can be checked carefully against the original.

POSTSCRIPT

JIM LYONS, of Mountain View, California, located the first printing of McDonald's ballad and sent me a photocopy. It ran under the title "The Volunteer," in the Sunday sports section of *The San Francisco Examiner*, July 26, 1908. A brief introduction to the poem points out that Thayer's original ballad (which the editors reprint) had appeared in the same paper in 1888, just twenty years earlier. A clipping from a New York newspaper, dated a few years after 1908, was sent to me by William R. Adams, of Manhattan; the two versions are identical.

As I surmised, the version I gave in the first edition of this book contained many errors. I have corrected them all. Except for a few trivial punctuation changes, and the substitution of "tall" for "short," the poem is now given as McDonald intended it.

CASEY—TWENTY YEARS LATER

The Bugville [1] team was surely up against a rocky game;
The chances were they'd win defeat and not undying
    fame;
Three men were hurt and two were benched; the score
    stood six to four.
They had to make three hard-earned runs in just two
    innings more.

"It can't be done," the captain said, a pallor on his face;
"I've got two pitchers in the field, a mutt [2] on second base;
And should another man get spiked or crippled in some
    way,
The team would sure be down and out, with eight men
    left to play.

"We're up against it anyhow as far as I can see;
My boys ain't hitting like they should and that's what
    worries me;
The luck is with the other side, no pennant will we win;
It's mighty tough, but we must take our medicine and
    grin."

The eighth round opened—one, two, three—the enemy
    went down.
The Bugville boys went out the same—the captain wore
    a frown.
The first half of the ninth came round, two men had been
    put out,
When Bugville's catcher broke a thumb and could not go
    the route.

A deathly silence settled o'er the crowd assembled there.
Defeat would be allotted them; they felt it in the air;
With only eight men in the field 'twould be a gruesome
    fray,—
Small wonder that the captain cursed the day he learned
    to play.

"Lend me a man to finish with!" he begged the other
    team;
"Lend you a man?" the foe replied; "My boy, you're in
    a dream!

We came to win the pennant, too—that's what we're doing
here.
There's only one thing you can do—call for a volunteer!"

The captain stood and pondered in a listless sort of way.
He never was a quitter and he would not be today!
"Is there within the grandstand here"—his voice rang loud
and clear—
"A man who has the sporting blood to be a volunteer?"

Again that awful silence settled o'er the multitude.
Was there a man among them with such recklessness
imbued?
The captain stood with cap in hand, while hopeless was
his glance,
And then a tall and stocky man cried out, "I'll take a
chance!"

Into the field he bounded with a step both firm and light;
"Give me the mask and mitt," he said; "let's finish up the
fight.
The game is now beyond recall; I'll last at least a round;
Although I'm ancient, you will find me muscular and
sound."

His hair was sprinkled here and there with little streaks
of gray;
Around his eyes and on his brow a bunch of wrinkles lay.
The captain smiled despairingly and slowly turned away.
"Why, he's all right!" one rooter yelled. Another, "Let
him play!"

"All right, go on," the captain sighed. The stranger turned
around,
Took off his coat and collar, too, and threw them on the
ground.
The humor of the situation seemed to hit them all,
And as he donned the mask and mitt, the umpire called,
"Play ball!"

Three balls the pitcher at him heaved, three balls of lightning speed.

The stranger caught them all with ease and did not seem
to heed.
Each ball had been pronounced a strike, the side had
been put out,
And as he walked in towards the bench, he heard the
rooters shout.

One Bugville boy went out on strikes, and one was killed
at first;
The captain saw them fail to hit, and gnashed his teeth
and cursed.
The third man smashed a double and the fourth man
swatted clear,
Then, in a thunder of applause, up came the volunteer.

His feet were planted in the earth, he swung a warlike
club;
The captain saw his awkward pose and softly whispered,
"Dub!" [3]
The pitcher looked at him and grinned, then heaved a
mighty ball;
The echo of that fearful swat still lingers with us all.

High, fast and far the spheroid flew; it sailed and sailed
away;
It ne'er was found, so it's supposed it still floats on today.
Three runs came in, the pennant would be Bugville's for
a year;
The fans and players gathered round to cheer the
volunteer.

"What is your name?" the captain asked. "Tell us your
name," cried all,
As down his cheeks great tears of joy were seen to run and
fall.
For one brief moment he was still, then murmured soft
and low:
"I'm mighty Casey who struck out just twenty years ago."

23. *LIKE KELLY DID*

by Clarence P. McDonald

Like Kelly Did is not about Casey, but it tells, in the meter and rhyme scheme of *Casey at the Bat,* the grim story of a member of the same Bugville team that Casey aided in McDonald's other poem. This is probably McDonald's revision of an earlier version that appears anonymously in *Around the World with the Baseball Bugs,* a booklet by Jack Regan and Will E. Stahl (Chicago: 1910), pp. 52-54.

LIKE KELLY DID

Bill Sweeney was a backstop on the mooted Bugville team;
At winging down to second base Bill Sweeney was a
dream.
The rooters used to swear by him, he was their joy and
pride,
Until he tried to emulate the famous "Kelly Slide." [1]

For Bill had seen this Kelly steal base after base and slide,
Had noted carefully his work, his manner, and his stride;
And Sweeney wished a thousand ways each time the
rooters cried,
They'd change the yell from Kelly and would screech,
"Slide, Sweeney, slide!"

But Kelly was a player with a wondrous burst of speed,
While Sweeney had a cracking whip but great speed
seemed to need;
And though he copied Kelly's style, when possible, and
slid,
The fans yelled: "Sweeney stole a base! He did? Like
Kelly did!"

For Sweeney was a moving van whene'er he reached a bag,
And when he tried to steal, his feet would tangle up and
lag;
And when he'd start, the fans would yelp together as a
man:
"O, Sweeney, he can steal a base! He can? Like Kelly can!"

Now, Sweeney was bullheaded, and he didn't seem to
know
He hadn't speed enough to beat the slowest kind of throw.
But Sweeney said that Kelly stole a base each time he slid,
And so he'd keep on trying till he stole—like Kelly did!

The Captain used to argue, and he'd say: "Now, look
here, Bill,
You never yet ain't stole no base, and what's more, never
will!

Mike Kelley, whose name was substituted for
Casey in many early printings of Thayer's ballad.

You're all right with you're throwin' arm, and with the
    mitt you're rare,
But when it comes to pilferin' the bags, why, you ain't
    there!

"Now, this here Kelly's got a speed our whole team can't
    attain,
And how this bunch cops out the games [2] is easy to
    explain;
But you—you've got to take a reef,[3] put out your stealin'
    flames,
Because your wild cavortin's costin' us a lot of games!"

Well, Bill was decent for awhile and played a ripping
    game,
He curbed his strong ambition to perpetuate his name;
And when he safely stung the pill and galloped down to
    first,
He'd hug the sack so closely that the Captain raved and
    cursed.

But when the shades of evening fell and the moon rose
    o'er the hill,
Bill sneaked out to the baseball lot and stole the bags
    at will.
He'd take a long lead off of first, then slide upon his shirt
For twenty feet, then stand on second and brush off the
    dirt.

At last the year drew to a close, the pennant season came,
And Bill was there behind the bat to play the final game.
"We'll take this fight," the Captain said to Bill, "and win
    the flag;
But for the love of all that's good, don't try to swipe a
    bag!"

The ninth round came; the visitors had tied the single
    score;
The side retired, the home boys came to bat amid a roar.
Bill opened with a double and was booted down to third;
Then rose the loudest rooting, Sweeney swore, he ever
    heard.

The next two died ere reaching first, and Bill was held on
    third;

Up stepped the heavy sticker [4] of the team—a clouting
    bird.
But while Bill pawed the ground at third, out yelled a
    zealous fan:
"O, Bill can steal home base and win! He can? Like
    Kelly can!"

Bill heard! Before his eyes there flashed a swift and livid
    flame!
At last the time was come to act—immortalize his name!
His moonlight practice had improved his speed—he'd sure
    make good!
He now was fleet as Kelly and could steal—like Kelly
    could!

And then, e'en while the pitcher held the ball, Bill sprang
    from third!
"Go back, you bonehead!" cried the boss, but Sweeney
    never heard.
A hush fell on the multitude—a silence deep, profound,
While Bill dived to the earth and plowed up twenty feet
    of ground!

In Bugville's potter's field today there is a little plot,
And o'er it stands a painted board which marks Bill's
    resting spot;
And those who run may read these words: "At last the
    fans are rid
Of Sweeney, who stole home and won! He did? Like
    Kelly did!"

24. CASEY—FORTY YEARS LATER

by Neil McConlogue

Casey—Twenty Years Later tells how a forty-eight-year-old Casey swatted a home run for Bugville. In 1927, the time of the game described in the following ballad, another twenty years have gone by and we find Casey, now sixty-eight, still capable of whacking the old pill out of the ball field. I have no notion of who Neil McConlogue might be. His prophetic poem appeared in *Baseball Magazine,* June, 1922, page 319, five years before the events it describes occurred.

CASEY—FORTY YEARS LATER

It's been forty years or thereabouts since Casey gained
    renown,
Because he couldn't clout the ball and knock it out of
    town.
The citizens of Mudville, who cheered that fateful day—
The young ones are all old folks and the old have passed
    away.

Now Bugville has a baseball team composed of faces new;
Of course there are no Cobbs or Ruths, it's a bush-league
    team, that's true.
So, I won't start criticizing the brand of ball they play,
I'm simply going to tell you what occurred the other day.

Now, I'm selling parts this summer for "the Hardly-
    Able" car—
It's the fastest thing on rubber, from Maine to Ballston
    Spa—[1]
When who should I meet, in Bugville, but my grand-sire,
    Hiram Bash,
With a pinchback[2] suit of linen and a freshly-bobbed
    mustache.

He had complimentary tickets for the game that after-
    noon—
And when it comes to baseball, I'm a bleacher-shoutin'
    loon.
It seems the Bugville "Acorns" were to play the Midvale[3]
    "Bears";
And the game would be a hummer and was sure to raise
    the hairs.

Most every fan in Bugville, as well as some "fanettes,"
Had put their hard-earned money up to satisfy their bets
That Midvale didn't have a chance with Bugville's hardy
    clan.
Oh! they backed the home team's chances, and they
    backed them to a man.

The innings came, the innings went, the seventh had gone
    by—

Five thousand throats in Bugville were tired, and very
dry;
While on the field the athletes played errorless and true,
And when the ninth had rolled around the score stood
two to two.

From the benches, black with people, there went up a
lusty roar.
The Midvale bunch had had their bat—and failed to
make a score.
Now a Bugville man makes second—No! "He's out," the
umpire said—
While five thousand tongues in Bugville showered curses
on his head.

Up from the home team's dug-out, a stranger to each fan,
There came, in ancient uniform, a sadly battered man
Whose hair had turned to silver; whose face was lined
and seamed,
But upon whose florid countenance determination
beamed.

The young fans didn't know him; the old ones there were
few.
But when grand-pa saw his profile—"right in the air he
flew";
For this sixty-eight-year batter was the often talked about,
The sturdy, Mighty Casey who had years before struck
out.

And now the pitcher holds the ball, and now he lets it go.
Alas, the air is shattered by the force of Casey's blow.
And far off on the outskirts, some two miles from the
game,
A baseball broke a window—also a window frame.

Oh! somewhere in this favored land the sun is shining
bright,
The fans are cheering someone—and a player's heart is
light.
For Mighty Casey's smiling, as he says he never knew
All the vigor he could garner from a goat gland that
was new! [4]

25. "COOL" CASEY
AT THE BAT

by the editors of *Mad*

THE following "hip" version of *Casey* was written by the staff of *Mad*. With wild illustrations by Don Martin, it first appeared in *Mad*, No. 26, October, 1960, and was reprinted in *The Self-Made Mad*, a 1964 Signet paperback. *Mad* had earlier run Thayer's original ballad, with equally wild illustrations that may be found in *The Bedside Mad*, a Signet paperback published in 1959. *"Cool" Casey at the Bat* is reprinted here with the permission of William Gaines, *Mad's* publisher, and is copyrighted © 1960 by E. C. Publications, Inc. Perhaps the reader can find a teen-ager who will translate it for him.

"COOL" CASEY AT THE BAT

The action wasn't groovy for the Endsville nine that day;
The beat was 4 to 2 with just one chorus more to sway.
And when old Cooney conked at first, and Barrows also
    sacked,
A nowhere rumble bugged up all the cats who dug the act.

A hassled group got all hung up and started in to split;
The other cats there played it cool and stayed to check the
    bit:
They figured if old Casey could, like, get in one more
    lick—
We'd put a lot of bread down, Man, on Casey and his
    stick!

But Flynn swung before Casey, and also Cornball Blake,
And the first stud didn't make it, and the other couldn't
    fake;
So the cats and all their chicks were dragged and in a
    bluesy groove,
For it was a sucker's long-shot that old Casey'd make his
    move.

But Flynn blew one cool single, and the hipsters did a flip,
And Blake, who was a loser, gave the old ball quite a trip;
And when the tempo let up, like a chorus played by Bird,
There was Cornball stashed at second and Flynn holed
    up at third.

Then from five thousand stomping cats there came a crazy
    sound;
It rocked all through the scene, Man—it really rolled
    around;
It went right to the top, Dad, and it charged on down
    below,
For Casey, swinging Casey—he was comin' on to blow!

There was style in Casey's shuffle as he came on with his
    stick;
There was jive in Casey's strutting; he was on a happy
    kick.

And when, to clue in all the cats, he doffed his lid real big,
The Square Johns in the group were hip: t'was Casey
    on the gig.

Ten thousand peepers piped him as he rubbed fuzz on
    his palms;
Five thousand choppers grooved it when he smeared some
    on his arms.
Then while the shook-up pitcher twirled the ball snagged
    in his clutch,
A hip look lit up Casey, Man, this cat was just too much!

And now the crazy mixed-up ball went flying out through
    space.
But Casey, he just eyed it with a cool look on his face.
Right at that charged-up sideman, the old ball really
    sailed—
"That's too far out," sang Casey. "Like, Strike One!" the
    umpire wailed.

From the pads stacked high with hipsters there was heard
    a frantic roar,
Like the beating of the bongos from a frenzied Be-Bop
    score,
"Knife him! Knife that ump, Man!" wailed some weirdo
    left-field clown;
And they would have cut the cat up, but cool Casey put
    them down.

With a real gone Beatnik grin on him, old Casey cooked
    with gas;
He fanned down all that ribble, and he sang, "On with
    this jazz!"
He set the pitcher straight, and once again the old ball
    flew;
But Casey wouldn't buy it and the ump howled, "Like,
    Strike Two!"

"He's sick!" wailed all the hipsters, and the Squares, too,
    sang out "Sick!"
But a nod from Daddy Casey, and those cats got off that
    kick.

They dug the way he sizzled, like his gaskets were of wax;
They were hip that Casey wouldn't let the ball get by his
ax.

The cool look's gone from Casey's chops, his eyes are all
popped up;
He stomps his big ax on the plate, he really is hopped up.
And now the pitcher cops the ball, and now it comes on
fast,
And now the joint is jumpin' with the sound of Casey's
blast.

Man, somewhere in this far-out scene the sun is packing
heat;
The group is blowing somewhere and somewhere guts
are beat,
And somewhere big cats break up, and small cats raise the
roof;
But there is no joy in Endsville—Swinging Casey made
a goof.

26. CASEY IN THE CAP

by J. A. Lindon

FOR many years J. A. Lindon, who lives near Weybridge, not far from London, has been writing some of the best comic verse in English. It is hard to come by, since much of it is written for weekly newspaper competitions—Lindon has often topped the winning lists—and seldom finds its way into anthologies. One of his finest parodies, *Poem in Tubwater* (a spoof of Dylan Thomas' *Poem in October*) is in *The Guinness Book of Poetry, 1958/59. Yet More Comic and Curious Verse,* selected by J. M. Cohen for Penguin Books (1959) contains his parodies of E. E. Cummings, T. E. Brown's *My Garden* ("A garden is a *lovesome* thing? What rot!"), Kipling's *If—,* and other delightful bits of nonsense. His marvelous *Fit the seven-and-a-half,* for Lewis Carroll's *Hunting of the Snark,* appears in my *Annotated Snark* (Simon & Schuster, 1962). Here are two unpublished Lindon parodies of *Casey.* First: a timely *Casey in the Cap,* annotated by the author.

CASEY IN THE CAP

Moon looked a rocky target to America that day:
Of late too many cosmonauts up there had lost their way;
And after James Scott Gussilpard [1] had vanished without
trace,
Taking Walter Edward Staffitt, there was tension at the
Base.

"It's a game of snakes-and-ladders,[2] life and prestige are
the stakes,
And you must keep mounting ladders, not come sliding
down the snakes,"
Mused Dr. William Lee. "Go wrong? With any other
chap.
But we shall soon be on the Moon with Casey in the cap!"

The mighty Saturn booster had sent roaring into space
The fifth Apollo capsule of the get-'em-up-there race;
And now, with lunar bug [3] attached and ready soon to
land,
In orbit round the Moon it lay with Casey in command.

First, Colonel Grissom Glenn McWhite had through the
tunnel crawled,
Then Schirra Young B. Carpenford had followed
unappalled;
A button sealed the hatches and the Lem [4] fell like a
glove,
To spiral swiftly moonward, leaving Casey up above.

He shot the message back to Base: "Decoupling gone
OK."
Cape Kennedy relayed it far beyond the USA:
On tellies by the million it went flashing round the earth,
Or crackling out of radios from Pontypool to Perth.[5]

Oh what a shout of human pride went up next from the
world!
What tears of joy and kissing! Oh the homburgs that were
hurled
Aloft to meet the ticker-tape when, shortly after noon,
The message came from Casey: "They have landed—on
the Moon!"

A hundred million misty eyes were focused on the sky
Or held in thrall by telly, fifty million throats were dry
As countdown for the blast-off of the lunar bug drew near
To "4-3-2-1-ZERO!" then "Ignition!" then "They're
clear!"

And Schirra Young B. Carpenford and Grissom Glenn
McWhite
Up from the lunar surface rose in pioneering flight
To where Commander Casey, very watchful now and
stern,
In orbit round the Moon would be awaiting their return

The Lem pursued Apollo, but the link-up didn't come,
For something must have happened—Casey's radio was
dumb;
The telly went on working, all could see (though it was
blurred)
That Casey *looked* attentive—but he didn't say a word!

Then over Casey's features came a sudden happy smile,
Which lulled the consternation of those watching—for a
while—
As gadgets all about him flickered "Link up!" from the
Lem,
And Casey *looked* attentive—but he wasn't heeding
them.

"God rot the guy!" exploded Lee. Cape Kennedy went
mad.
A hundred million eyes on earth could see that things
were bad
As Schirra Young B. Carpenford and Grissom Glenn
McWhite
Tried for their third and final link, then vanished—into
Night.

The smile is gone from Casey's lip, his eyes are bulging
out,
His tongue goes licking to and fro, he would not hear a
shout . . .

Excitedly he turns a page, ejaculates "Gee whizz!"
He is reading Science Fiction, he's forgotten where he is!

Oh somewhere two poor cosmonauts are flying through
   the void,
Both feeling most uneasy lest they meet an asteroid;
And somewhere they may light on one—and perish with
   a slap—
But never they'll link up again with Casey in the cap.

27. *A VILLAGE CRICKET CASEY*

by J. A. Lindon

LINDON's second parody, *A Village Cricket Casey,* tells the story of Casey in terms that only the English can understand. The notes are the author's.

I must add that Mr. Lindon is an authority on English word play and one of the world's leading palindromists. (See his contributions to the notes of C. C. Bombaugh, *Oddities and Curiosities of Words and Literature,* a Dover paperback.) He recently tried his hand on some Casey palindromes. Here are two of them:

Yes, a call, a bat, a ball, a Casey!

Won't I help? Miss it in mad stab? Yes, a Casey bats. Damn! It is simple—hit *now*.

A VILLAGE CRICKET CASEY

It had been a sticky wicket at Cowpat-under-Slosh,
A day of storm and sunshine, of heat and mackintosh;
And now, 6 down for 39, they feared that they must lose
To the visiting eleven from Mudlark-in-the-Ooze.

They needed only 50, but their play was out-of-joint,
For Joe Darke, who was Sexton, spooned a dolly-catch to
    point,
And little "Bunny" Scutters was bowled around his legs
By a ball that pitched a yard wide—then broke, and took
    his pegs.

Thin Skinne came in with Blockham: there were jabs
    and Chinese cuts [1]
(Tail-enders both—good bowlers, but they couldn't bat
    for nuts);
So hopes were pinned on Casey, "Hard" Casey from the
    forge:
An iron-muscled blacksmith, he could *hit* the ball, by
    George!

Skinne hooked a lucky single, then Blockham flicked a
    four,
Which meant that six were needed to make the winning
    score.
Schoolmaster hollered, Shepherd bleated, Parson waved
    his beer,
And Wally Thatcher, up a tree, fell plop! into the weir.

Then Blockham thought he'd 'have a go'—the Umpire
    came to put
The bails back on his shattered stumps—he'd missed it by
    a foot!
And the shocked and awful silence that greeted his decease
Became a yell, for Casey was advancing to the crease.

Grim-smiling and determined, he came striding up the
    pitch
Like a mighty Alec Bedser (maybe Eric,[2] who knows
    which?);
He sported no white flannels, he scorned to wear a cap,
But in dungarees, bare-chested, he stood to fill the gap.

A hundred eyes were on him, even goats there on the
   green
Stopped grazing for a moment, said "Maaahh!" when
   they had seen
The Umpire give him centre, which he marked with
   heavy thumps . . .
Then, standing up, he scrutinised the field about his
   stumps.

Behind him crouched the keeper, as bald as any egg—
(The Mudlark village grocer), slip, gully, backward leg;
Before him only cover; the rest were on the ropes
Awaiting lofty mis-hits from this man of Cowpat's hopes.

Now he is hunched and ready. The bowler, with a cough,
Slings down a ball that curves away, then nips in from
   the off;
And Casey whirls a mighty bat which doesn't quite
   connect,
And everybody gulps to see his wicket still erect.

The bowler licks his finger, flips back his hair, and comes
Jig-hopping up to bowl again. The spinning leather hums
And dips and bounces on the pitch where ducks [3] can be
   a scandal,
And Casey swipes at it so hard his blade flies off the
   handle!

Good Parson now is praying, Schoolmaster dare not look,
Old Shepherd unawares has tied a sheepshank in his
   crook;
All know if Casey should connect he'll score the winning
   clout,
But if he misses once again most likely he'll be out.

Another bat is brought him. His blade taps in the
   block [4] . . .
A golden note comes belling from the old church-tower
   clock . . .
The bowler whips the leather down, all wait for victory,
And even Wally Thatcher has found another tree.

Oh what a SHOUT of TRIUMPH as the wicket fails to
  fall!
Oh what a SHOUT of TRIUMPH at the sound of bat
  on ball!
Oh what a SHOUT—from Mudlark—as Casey, moved by
  care,
Prods with excessive caution, and pops it in the air!

28. O'TOOLE'S TOUCHDOWN

by Les Desmond

IT WAS inevitable, I suppose, that someone would parody *Casey* in terms of football. *O'Toole's Touchdown* was recorded by De Wolf Hopper on the reverse side of one of his Victor recordings of *Casey* (see Note 5, *There Was Ease in Casey's Manner* . . .). The label says it was written by Les Desmond, about whom I have uncovered nothing. I have cleaned up some of the lines in which the meter stumbled, either because of the writer's carelessness or Hopper's faulty memory. Unfortunately, as in the case of *The Man Who Fanned Casey,* there is no known printed version of the poem with which the recorded version can be compared.

O'TOOLE'S TOUCHDOWN

The outlook wasn't brilliant for the Hokus[1] team that
    day;
The score was three to nothing with two minutes more
    to play.
And so when Cohen lost five yards, and Zipkin did the
    same,
A sickly silence fell upon the patrons of the game.

A straggling few got up to go in deep despair, the rest
Clung to the hope that springs eternal in the human
    breast;
They thought if only Mike O'Toole[2] was out there on
    the field,
That fact might be enough to cause the other side to yield.

But Mighty Mike O'Toole was out; his left arm had been
    broken.
He hadn't been in any game since Hokus played
    Shemoken.[3]
So on that stricken multitude grim melancholy sat.
A touchdown now would win the game, though who
    dared hope for that?

But ten yards were gained by Cohen, to the wonderment
    of all,
And Metza ran another ten before he downed the ball!
And when the dust had lifted and they saw what had been
    done,
Hokus was in midfield with but fifty yards to run!

Then from five thousand throats and more went up a
    lusty yell;
It rumbled in the valley, it rattled in the dell;
It knocked upon the mountain top, and to the ear
    re-pealed,
For O'Toole, Mighty Mike O'Toole, was trotting on the
    field!

There was ease in O'Toole's manner as he stepped into
    his place;
There was pride in O'Toole's bearing and a smile on
    O'Toole's face.

And when responding to the cheers he waved his good
   right palm,
No stranger doubted, 'twas O'Toole who stood there cool
   and calm.

Ten thousand eyes were on him as he dug his cleats in
   dirt;
Five thousand tongues applauded for they knew that he'd
   been hurt.
And as lower crouched the center, ready the ball to flip,
Defiance gleamed in O'Toole's eye, a sneer curled
   O'Toole's lip.

But ere the leather-covered ball came hurtling through
   the air,
O'Toole was leaping forward from his haughty grandeur
   there.
The whistle blew! Ole Hokus, five more yards was
   penalized;
Just that much farther from the goal, the thing so dearly
   prized.

From the benches black with people there went up a
   muffled roar,
Like the beating of the storm waves on a stern and distant
   shore.
"Kill that blamed official!" shouted someone on the stand,
And it's likely they'd have killed him had not O'Toole
   raised his hand.

With a smile of Christian charity great O'Toole's visage
   shone;
He stilled the rising tumult, he bade the game go on.
The line crouched low, the quarterback his rapid signals
   gave;
The ball snapped back, the line held firm, it didn't even
   cave.

But look! It is a forward pass from quarter to O'Toole!
The Mighty Mike has grabbed it; he has started for the
   goal!
With ball clutched firmly to his breast, he speeds with
   bound on bound.
He flies across the goal line, and then drops to the ground.

Oh, somewhere men are laughing, and children shout
  with glee;
And somewhere bands are playing, and somewhere hearts
  are free.
And somewhere in this favored land the glorious sun
  does shine,
But there is no joy in Hokus, O'Toole crossed the wrong
  goal line!

29. *AHAB AT THE HELM*

by Ray Bradbury

RAY BRADBURY, one of the most admired of all authors of modern science fiction and fantasy, wrote the screenplay for John Huston's celebrated production of *Moby Dick,* with Gregory Peck as the mad Captain Ahab. A few years later, *Ahab at the Helm* seemed to write itself. It was first published in *Connoisseur's World* in 1964 and has since been reprinted in various periodicals, though it is not in any of Bradbury's books. The author received a standing ovation in November, 1969, when he recited the ballad during his lecture on "Creativity in the Space Age," at the University of California, Los Angeles. Admirers of *Moby Dick* will recognize the poem's many literary allusions, not to mention its skillful echoes of Thayer's ballad.

AHAB AT THE HELM

It looked extremely rocky for the Melville nine that day,
The score stood at two lowerings, with one lowering yet to
 play,
And when Fedallah died and rose, and others did the same
A pallor wreathed the features of the patrons of this Game.

A straggling few downed-oars to go, leaving behind the
 rest,
With that hope which springs eternal from the blind dark
 human breast.
They prayed that Captain Ahab's rage would thrust,
 strike, overwhelm!
They'd wager "Death to Moby!" with old Ahab at the
 helm.

But Flask preceded Ahab, and likewise so did Stubb,
And the former was a midget, while the latter was a nub.
Behold! the stricken multitudes in silence pent did swoon,
For when, oh when would Ahab rise to hurl his dread
 harpoon? !

First Flask let drive a gaffing hook. The wonderment of all!
Then much-despised Stubb's right arm brought blood and
 bile and gall!
But when the mist had lifted, Ishmael saw what had
 occurred:
Flask stood safe in the second boat, while Stubb clutched
 to the third.

Then from the gladdened whaling-men went up a joyous
 yell,
It bounded from the tidal hills and echoed in the dell,
It struck upon the soaring wave, shook Pequod's mast and
 keel,
For Ahab, mighty Ahab, was advancing with his steel.

There was ease in Ahab's manner as he stepped into his
 place,
There was pride in Ahab's bearing and a smile on Ahab's
 face;
The cheers, the wildest shoutings, did not him overwhelm,

No man in all that crowd could doubt, 'twas Ahab at the
helm.

Four dozen eyes fixed on him as he coiled the hempen rope,
Two dozen tongues applauded as he raised his steel, their
hope.
And while the writhing Moby ground the whale-boats
with his hip,
Defiance gleamed from Ahab's eye, a sneer curled Ahab's
lip.

And now the white-fleshed monster came a-hurtling
through the air,
While Ahab stood despising it in haughty grandeur there!
Close by the sturdy harpooner the Whale unheeded sped—
"That ain't my style," said Ahab. "Strike! Strike!" Good
Starbuck said.

From the longboats black with sailors there uprose a sullen
roar,
Like the beating of mad storm waves on a stern and distant
shore:
"Kill Starbuck! Kill the First Mate!" shouted someone of
the band.
And its likely they'd have done so had not Ahab raised
his hand.

With a smile of Christian charity great Ahab's visage
shone,
He stilled the rising tumult and he bade the Chase go on.
He signalled to the White Whale, and again old Moby
flew.
But still Ahab ignored it. Ishmael cried, "Strike! Strike,
man!" too.

"Fraud!" yelled the rebel sailors, and sea-echoes answered,
"Fraud!"
But one scornful glance from Ahab and his audience was
awed.
They saw his face grow pale and cold, they saw his muscles
strain,
And they knew that Ahab's fury would not pass that
Whale again.

The sneer is gone from Ahab's lips, his teeth are clenched in hate,
He pounds with cruel violence his harpoon upon his pate,
And now old Moby gathers power, and now he lets it go.
And now the air is shattered by the force of Ahab's blow!

Oh, somewhere on the Seven Seas, the sun is shining bright,
The hornpipe plays yet somewhere and somewhere hearts are light;
And somewhere teachers laugh and sing, and somewhere scholars shout,
But there is no joy in Melville—mighty Ahab has Struck Out.

NOTES

INTRODUCTION

1. Some other one-poem poets: Clement C. Moore, *A Visit from St. Nicholas* (and Robert L. May who wrote its sequel, *Rudolph the Red-Nosed Reindeer*); Sam Walter Foss, *The House by the Side of the Road;* Arthur Chapman, *Out Where the West Begins;* Samuel Woodworth, *The Old Oaken Bucket;* Adelaide Proctor, *The Lost Chord.* For the story of *Evolution,* by one-poem poet Langdon Smith, see my article "When You Were a Tadpole and I Was a Fish," in *Antioch Review,* Vol. 22 (Fall, 1962), pp. 332-340. Burton Stevenson discusses fifteen such poems (including *Casey*) in *Famous Single Poems* (Harcourt, Brace and Co., 1923). There are also one-line poets, such as John William Burgon, a prolific nineteenth-century poet who is remembered today for only one line—"A rose-red city half as old as Time." And one must not forget Billings, the no-poem poet in Mark Twain's *Captain Stormfield's Visit to Heaven,* whose poetry rivaled Homer's and Shakespeare's, but no one would print it.

THERE WAS EASE IN CASEY'S MANNER . . .

1. In an interview with Homer Croy (see bibliography) Thayer is quoted as saying that in the fall of 1887 he had been reading W. S. Gilbert's *Bab Ballads,* and they had prompted him to attempt similar ballads for his newspaper column. *Casey* was written, Thayer said, in May, 1888. He received five dollars for each ballad.

2. In his memoirs, Hopper gives the date as May 13, 1888. This is certainly incorrect because *Casey* was not printed in the *San Francisco Examiner* until June 3 of that year. Hopper also wrongly recalls that the initials "E.L.T." were appended to the ballad. In *Famous Single Poems,* Burton Stevenson says he received a letter from Hopper correcting the date given in his memoirs and stating his conviction that the historic first recitation of *Casey* was in August, 1888. Thanks to the diligent research of Jules L. Levitt, of Binghamton, New York, this has now been verified. A review in *The New York Times,* August 15, 1888, page 4, describes the memorable occasion on the night of August 14 when Hopper gave his first recitation of *Casey,* and how it was "uproariously received" by the audience.

3. See Note 1 on Grantland Rice's poem, *The Man Who Played with Anson on the Old Chicago Team.*

4. William ("Buck") Ewing, catcher for the New York Giants. He is said to have been the first catcher to throw to second without wasting time by standing up. On one famous occasion he stole second, then third, shouted out that he intended to steal home, which he did. Robert Smith, in his recent picture book *Baseball's Hall of Fame* (Bantam, 1965), says that a lithograph depicting Ewing's mighty slide, as he stole home, was widely sold all over New York City. In 1883 Buck led the National League in home runs.

5. Hopper's deep, rich voice, reciting *Casey,* was first recorded in 1906 on a Victor Grand Prize Record, No. 31559. This was reissued in 1913 as No. 35290, with a reverse side bearing *The Man Who Fanned Casey,* recited by Digby Bell, a popular singing comedian of the day. A new recording of Hopper doing *Casey* was released by Victor in 1926 as "orthophonic recording" No. 35783. On the flip side Hopper recited the parody, *O'Toole's Touchdown.* Perhaps Hopper made other recordings of *Casey,* but these three are all I could find. A garbled version of *Casey,* cluttered with sound effects and corny music, was recorded much later by Lionel Barrymore on two sides of an M.G.M. record. A recent recording by Mel Allen is on a Golden Record for children.

6. See Note 5 on Rice's poem, *The Man Who Played with Anson on the Old Chicago Team.*

7. This production, with Louis Venora as the mute Casey, was by the Julius Hartt Opera Guild. In addition to *The New York Times* review mentioned later, see also reviews in *Time* (Vol. 60, May 18, 1953, p. 61) and *Musical America* (Vol. 73, June, 1953).

8. The Omnibus show featured Danny Scholl as Casey, Elise Rhodes as Merry. A preview, with pictures, appeared in the *New York Herald Tribune,* March 4, 1955. Harold C. Schonberg reviewed the Omnibus show for *The New York Times,* March 7, 1955.

9. This ballad (in Eliot's *Old Possum's Book of Practical Cats,* Harcourt, Brace and Co., 1939) relates the fall of the great, one-eyed pirate cat, Growltiger, "The Terror of the Thames." Growltiger pursues his evil aims by roaming up and down the river on a barge. But one balmy moonlit night, when his barge is anchored at Molesey and his raffish crew members are either

asleep or wetting their beards at nearby pubs, he is cornered by a gang of Siamese cats and, to his vast surprise, forced to walk the plank:

> He who a hundred victims had driven to that drop,
> At the end of all his crimes was forced to go ker-flip, ker-flop.

The ballad's fourteen stanzas follow the rhyme scheme and iambic septameter of *Casey*. The final stanza begins: "Oh there was joy in Wapping . . ." [Wapping, on the Thames, is a dreary dock section of Stepney, an eastern borough of London. Its inhabitants—mostly longshoremen, sailors, and factory hands— are called Wappingers. Boswell writes of an occasion on which Samuel Johnson talked about "the wonderful extent and variety of London, and observed, that men of curious inquiry might see in it such modes of life as very few could even imagine. He in particular recommended to us to *explore Wapping* . . ." This Boswell did. But he adds: ". . . whether from that uniformity which has in modern times, in a great degree, spread through every part of the Metropolis, or from our want of sufficient exertion, we were disappointed."]

10. Santayana, *Persons and Places* (Scribner's, 1943), page 197. Santayana's failure to mention *Casey* may be accounted for, in part, by the fact that he greatly preferred football to baseball.

11. These remarks of Thayer's are quoted in his obituary in the *Santa Barbara* (California) *News-Press*, August 22, 1940.

1. CASEY AT THE BAT, first printing, by Ernest L. Thayer

1. In 1887, the year of the immortal game, Mudville was a farming village near the east border of Anderson County, Kansas, about sixty miles southeast of Topeka. It was on the south bank of Polecat Creek, seven miles west of where Centerville, in Linn County, is still located. Neither Mudville nor the creek exist today.

The poignant story of why and how Mudville faded from the map is told by Grantland Rice in his poem, *Mudville's Fate*. In early 1902, in a futile effort to change its image, Mudville's civic leaders had the town's name officially changed to Moorville, but residents of the area refused to call it that and the town continued to deteriorate rapidly. By 1907 it had disappeared entirely and Casey, with his wife and eight children, had moved to nearby Bugville. Like Podunk, another American town that no longer exists, Mudville has become a slang term of derision for the hick town. It should not be confused with Mudlick, Ky., Mud Butte, S. Dak., Mudfork, W. Va., Muddy Creek Forks, Pa., Muddy, Ill., Mud Camp, Ky., or Mud, Ill.

Below the original printing of the ballad, the following note (probably written by Thayer) appears: "When they talked about the nine in ancient Athens it was the nine Muses; to-day, all over the country, the nine refers to baseball, excepting through the Middle and Western States, where it is understood to mean quinine."

The Mudville Nine, as recorded in *The Mighty Casey*, consisted of: Pitcher: Andy Jones, Catcher: Red O'Toole, First Base: Otis Barrows, Second Base: Tony Perrone, Third Base: Jimmy Blake, Shortstop: Scooter Cooney, Left Field: Roughhouse Flynn, Center Field: Benny Rabensky, Right Field: Casey.

The libretto does not give Casey's first and middle names. Brian Kavanagh Casey was born at Mudville on August 4, 1859, the son of John Casey, plumber, and Mary O'Toole. His mother was the aunt of Red O'Toole, the catcher on Casey's team. (The ballad *O'Toole's Touchdown* tells the story of a later episode involving Red's son Michael when he played on the Hokus College football team.) The year 1859 was, in many lesser respects, a momentous one. Among other things, it was the year John Brown was hanged, Karl Marx published his *Critique of Political Economy*, Charles Darwin published *The Origin of Species*, John Stuart Mill published his treatise *On Liberty*, Richard Wagner finished *Tristan*, *Dixie* was composed by minstrel Dan Emmett, and the world's first oil well was drilled in Titusville, Pa. It was the year of birth for philosophers John Dewey, Henri Bergson, Samuel Alexander, and Edmund Husserl, as well as for Conan Doyle, A. E. Houseman, Havelock Ellis, Pierre Curie, and the Kaiser.

"That day," the day of the immortal game, was Saturday, September 3, 1887. Casey was twenty-eight.

2. Scooter Cooney, shortstop. He is a hired hand for farmer Tuthill. (*The Mighty Casey*, page 45.) "Died at first" means, of course, that Cooney was caught out at first base.

3. Otis Barrows, first base; a second-year Volunteer Fire Chief and son of the man who runs Mudville's barbershop. (*The Mighty Casey*, page 43. Throughout the libretto his name is incorrectly spelled "Burrows.")

4. The line is from Pope's *Essay on Man*, Epistle III:

> Hope springs eternal in the human breast:
> Man never is, but always to be blest.

5. We learn from *The Mighty Casey* (page 49) that Casey's batting average for the season is .564. He has knocked in two hundred runs and hit ninety-nine homers. A home run now would hit the hundred mark. In the opera's première Casey was incorrectly played as a southpaw; actually, he threw and batted right-handed.

6. Peter ("Roughhouse") Flynn, left field. A good hitter, but during the season he has been benched eleven times and fined seven times for insulting the umpire. (*The Mighty Casey*, page 46.)

7. James Elmer Blake, third base. By day he plays baseball, at night—as Bobo Blake, leader of the Mudville Melodians—he plays dance music. (*The Mighty Casey*, page 44.)

8. Lulu: Something extraordinary, a humdinger. Here used in a derisive sense.

9. Cake: A slang word of the time for a dude, dandy, or male homosexual. Here it probably means no more than a handsome, vain ball player, much concerned about his personal appearance, but a weak player.

10. Baseball hyperbole, not to be taken literally. But compare with the episode in Bernard Malamud's *The Natural* (1952)— the novel is a mad and melancholy elaboration of the *Casey* myth—in which the mighty Roy Hobbs is told by his manager to knock the cover off the ball, and he does:

> Wonderboy [Roy's homemade bat] flashed in the sun. It caught the sphere where it was biggest. A noise like a twenty-one gun salute cracked the sky. There was a straining, ripping sound . . . The ball screamed toward the pitcher and seemed suddenly to dive down at his feet. He grabbed it to throw to first and realized to his horror that he held only the cover. The rest of it, unraveling cotton thread as it rode, was headed into the outfield.
> Roy was rounding first when the ball plummeted like a dead bird into center field. Attempting to retrieve and throw, the Philly fielder got tangled in thread. The second baseman rushed up, bit the cord and heaved the ball to the catcher but Roy had passed third and made home, standing. The umpire called him safe and immediately a rhubarb boiled.

11. And the men: The word "the" is so disruptive of the line's rhythm that it must surely have been inserted inadvertently by the printer. Thayer removed it from his revised version of 1909. Other versions correct the meter by substituting "they" for "the men."

12. Johnnie: A printer's mistake. It should have been Jimmy.

13. The Centerville pitcher is James Riley Snedeker, known as "Fireball." A Centerville spy (as we learn in *The Mighty Casey*, p. 21f) has informed Thatcher, the Centerville catcher, that Casey's one weakness is a high, inside ball. Fireball and Thatcher have agreed on a secret signal for such a pitch: Thatcher is to scratch his left ear. When Fireball later went to Boston, to pitch for the Beaneaters, he changed his last name to Riley. For his reason, see the introduction to *Riley in the Box*.

14. At this point *The Mighty Casey* interpolates a new stanza:

The cheering then diminished and the hucksters' raucous shout
Was quickly met by threats and cries of "Quiet—throw them out!"
At last the throng fell silent and the barking hawkers quit—
And the only sound was the catcher's hand pounding the catcher's mitt.

15. The umpire's last name (*The Mighty Casey*, page 122) is Buttenheiser. He is a man of irreproachable judgment and exact vision.

16. *Cf.,* the opening lines of Felicia Dorothea Hemans' *The Landing of the Pilgrim Fathers:*

The breaking waves dashed high
On a stern and rock-bound coast,

17. Between this stanza and the next, *The Mighty Casey* inserts the following:

The pitcher moves with caution, his eyes then sweep the field,
The catcher's hand then gives a sign, the pact between them sealed.
The pitcher knows his signals, he's been taught by plotting brains.
A high and inside ball 't'will be—for a single strike remains.

18. *No Joy in Mudville* (Schenkman, 1965) is the title of a book by Ralph Andreano, an economist at Earlham College. The book discusses reasons for the recent decline of public interest in big league baseball; it recommends that management find

ways of re-creating such "folk heroes" as Casey and King Kelly instead of the colorless, faceless "organization men" that are typical of today's major league players.

19. To "pull a Casey" or "do a Casey" is now a common baseball colloquialism for a strike out at a crucial moment.

2. *CASEY AT THE BAT,* an early corrupted version, by Ernest L. Thayer

1. A shortened form of "pudding-head." (*Cf.,* Mark Twain's *Puddin'head Wilson.*) A stupid but lovable person. In later printings of *Casey,* the word was usually contracted to "puddin'." Many other derogatory words have been substituted here for Thayer's original "lulu" (and his later "hoodoo"); for example, it is "no-good" in the version of *Casey* that appears in Edward Branch Lyman's *Baseball Fanthology,* 1924.

3. *CASEY AT THE BAT,* revised version by Ernest L. Thayer

1. And so when (1900).

2. grim despair (1900).

3. With that hope which springs eternal in every human breast (1900).

4. Stayed thinking "if great Casey could but get a whack at that" (1900).

5. Hoodoo: Someone who brings bad luck. (See Don Fairbairn's *Why Casey Whiffed.*)

6. "Dat ain't my style," (1900).

7. stern but distant shore (1900).

8. "Kill him, kill de umpire," (1900).

9. and again (1900). Mark Sullivan, in his *Our Times,* prints a corrupted version of *Casey* in which this line reads: "He signaled to Sir Timothy, once more the spheroid flew." We know Sir Timothy is pitching for New York because in stanza 7 of this version "the writhing pitcher" is changed to "the New York pitcher," but whether there was a New York pitcher then called Sir Timothy, I do not know. Sullivan states in a footnote that he did his best to obtain the ballad's authorized version, and that Hopper assured him in a letter that although "millions" had claimed the poem, its real author was one Ernest T. Thayer.

10. The sneer is fled (1900).

4. *CASEY'S REVENGE,* first book printing, by Grantland Rice

1. I have not been able to pin down the precise sense in which Rice used the word "shine." That it was common baseball slang

in 1910, at least in the south, is evident from Rice's use of it in other poems in his *Base-Ball Ballads*. The word was then, as well as now, usually a disparaging term for a Negro, but from time to time it has had other connotations. For example, in George Vere Hobart's short novel, *It's up to You* (1902), it is clearly (page 11) a slang term for being effeminate. At times it has simply been a vague term of disparagement, like the word "bum," and probably was used by Rice in that sense. Note that he substitutes the word "punk" in his later revision of the ballad.

2. Hit the second: Hit the second batter with the ball, thus giving him a walk to first.

5. *CASEY'S REVENGE*, revised version, by Grantland Rice

1. An inferior, worthless player.

2. Clucks: Dopes, dunces.

3. Pinches: critical situations.

4. Tony Perrone, second base. See Thayer's original version, Note 1.

5. Pete: Peter ("Roughhouse") Flynn. See Note 6 of Thayer's first version.

6. *MUDVILLE'S FATE*, by Grantland Rice

1. Dog fennel: Mayweed. A strongly scented weed of the aster family, with yellow flowers.

2. "Whiffing" is an old baseball expression for striking out. Any swing that misses the ball, in both golf and baseball, is also called a "whiff."

3. James Winter, the blacksmith, moved to Chicago. Caleb Perley, the druggist (see *The Mighty Casey*, page 4), settled in Tulsa, Oklahoma.

4. Biffed: Struck. Casey whiffed by biffing the air instead of the ball.

7. *THE MAN WHO PLAYED WITH ANSON ON THE OLD CHICAGO TEAM,* by Grantland Rice

1. Adrian Constantine ("Pop") Anson managed the Chicago White Stockings (the name later became the Chicago Cubs) from 1879 to 1897. A strapping six-footer, "Cap" Anson ("Cap" for Captain became "Pop" with the passing years) played every position on the team until he finally settled at first base to become the most famous "playing manager" of his day and one of the strongest sluggers in the big leagues. He was in the majors for twenty-seven seasons (no one has been in the majors for a longer period), played 2,250 games, and had a lifetime batting average of .337.

"He was known in every city of the country," writes Lee Allen in his chapter on "The Glory Years of Anson" (*The National League Story,* Hill & Wang, 1961). "Small boys bought Anson-model bats and treasured them as their most prized possessions. . . . Until Babe Ruth, he was the most widely known player in the game." Anson was the first ball player to write an autobiography: *A Ball Player's Career* (Chicago: Era Publishing Co., 1900).

2. A town in Kankakee County, northeast Illinois.

3. Probably Pikeville, Indiana, though there are other Pikevilles in Kentucky, North Carolina, and Tennessee.

4. Edward N. Williamson, White Stockings shortstop, was another great Chicago batsman. His twenty-seven home runs in 1884 was the record until Babe Ruth broke it in 1919. "Ed was, in my opinion, the greatest all-round ballplayer the country ever saw," wrote Anson in his autobiography (p. 113). "After his retirement from the diamond he ran a saloon in company with Jimmy Woods, another ballplayer, on Dearborn Street, Chicago, which was a popular resort for the lovers of sport."

5. Michael ("Mike") Joseph Kelly, known as "King" Kelly, was one of the brightest stars of Anson's great team. He was the most colorful, on and off the field, of all major league players before 1900; surely the greatest ham in the history of baseball. He usually caught or played outfield. In his early days, when he made a successful catch in the field he sometimes turned a somersault before throwing back the ball. He batted right handed, his left hand at the end of the bat, his right hand halfway up the wood as if intending to bunt. Just before swinging he would slide the right hand down. His fantastic base-running

skill inspired the yell "Slide, Kelly, Slide!" It was the title of a popular song about him in the 1880's and, in 1927, the name of a silent M-G-M motion picture starring William Haines.

So many stories were told about King Kelly that it is hard to separate truth from myth. The following best authenticated stories are from Alfred P. Cappio's valuable monograph: "Slide, Kelly, Slide," published by the Passaic County Historical Society (Lambert Castle, Patterson 3, New Jersey) and currently available for fifty cents.

Once when Kelly was managing the Boston team, and coaching from third base, he insisted on inspecting the ball. But when the pitcher tossed it to him, he stepped aside. As the ball rolled away, a runner stole second. On another occasion Kelly leaped from the bench, shouted "Kelly now catching for Boston!" and grabbed a foul pop fly. This led to a change in the official rules, writes Cappio, which had stated that a manager could make a substitution "at any point in the game." During a game that had gone into extra innings and was about to be called because of darkness, Kelly made some sort of fantastic outfield catch that ended the game. Later, he confessed that the ball had not even touched his glove; he had only *pretended* to catch it. If, while running bases, he saw that an umpire's eyes were elsewhere, he would cut a base by as much as fifteen feet. It is said that he once scored from first without coming even close to second or third.

Kelly's most incredible exploit occurred when he was on Anson's Chicago team, playing in Detroit. It was the ninth inning, score tied, one out. Mike reached first on a hit, then Ed Williamson got a base on balls. The pair executed a successful double steal. Mike picked himself up at third, clutching his arm and howling with pain. "Everyone, including Williamson, rushed over to see what was wrong," writes Cappio. "Between groans, Kelly whispered instructions into Big Ed's ear. Suddenly Mike broke for home. The Detroit players came alive and threw the ball to the catcher in plenty of time to get Kelly out. Just as he reached the plate, Mike stopped short and spread his legs wide apart. As the catcher touched Mike out, Williamson, who had closely followed Kelly home, dived safely through the outstretched legs and scored the winning run."

Whether these tales be true or not, there is no doubt that Kelly was one of the most creative rascals in professional ball. Anson credited him with having invented the hit and run play. Cappio says he was the first catcher to signal to the outfielders what the pitcher intended to throw next, and the first to suggest that pitcher and catcher back up basemen to snag possible overthrows. He did not invent the slide, but he knew all the tricks later used by Ty Cobb, including some which, says Cappio, have never been imitated. "His big body would hurl itself toward the base amid a cloud of dust, and the baseman would stab at one of Kelly's feet only to find the other foot securely hooked to the bag."

The King was a tall, good-looking Irishman, with an enormous black mustache of the handlebar variety. Off the field, his fancy clothes, his passion for the horses and hard liquor, made continuous newspaper copy. "Money slipped through Mike's fingers as water slips through the meshes of a fisherman's net," wrote Anson, in his autobiography (p. 195), "and he was as fond of whisky as any representative of the Emerald Isle . . ." In 1888—the year *Casey* was first printed—Kelly was managing the Boston team, having been sold for the then-unheard-of price of $10,000. "The ten thousand dollar beauty," the papers called him. During 1887, his first year with Boston, his batting average was .394—the highest he ever achieved—and he stole eighty-four bases. So great was his fame in 1888 that a Boston publisher, Emery and Hughes, brought out his autobiography: an eighty-six page paperback (now rare) called *Play Ball: Stories of the Diamond Field.* Little wonder that in the summer of 1888, when newspapers began reprinting *Casey,* they changed the name to Kelly and the locale to Boston.

Those early Kelly versions of *Casey* proved prophetic, for the King soon began a tragic downward slide. He would show up for games in an alcoholic stupor and, after misjudging an easy fly, would exclaim, "By Gad, I made it hit me glove!" Running bases, he sometimes tripped over his feet and fell on his face. Boston sent him to Cincinnati, Cincinnati shoved him back to Boston, and Boston passed him on to the New York Giants. The Giants, Cappio tells us, tried to sober him up in a Turkish bath before each game. But one afternoon, when he failed to report, they discovered that he had passed up the bath for a visit to a nearby saloon, and had then taken a bottle with him to the race track. The Giants sent him back to Boston, but Boston didn't want him either.

He ended in the minors, managing the Allentown, Pennsylvania, team. During his better days he had often spent his off-season months as a well paid but hammy actor in Broadway plays. But his best performances, writes Cappio, were in hotel barrooms where his recitations of *Casey at the Bat,* with appropriate gestures, were said to surpass even those of De Wolf

Hopper. As the boozing increased he had to leave the legitimate stage for specialty acts in vaudeville and burlesque houses. In October, 1894, after a year of drunken play with the Allentown team, he showed up in Paterson, New Jersey, his home town, with Mike Murphy's burlesque troupe. From the stage of the Bijou Theatre, the mighty King Kelly recited *Casey*. He was booked into Boston. But a cold turned into pneumonia, and as he was being carried through a Boston hospital door on a stretcher, he slipped to the floor whispering (it is said) "This is my last slide." On November 8—flat broke and thirty-seven years old—Mike Kelly died. He had heard, said a Boston newspaper obituary, "the decision of the Great Umpire from which there is no appeal."

"Baseball and booze will not mix any better than will oil and water," wrote Anson in his autobiography. "He died . . . a victim to fast living and a warning to all ball players. Had he been possessed of good habits instead of bad there is no telling to what heights Kelly might have climbed, for a better fellow in some respects never wore a baseball uniform."

For more on Kelly, see: *"Slide, Kelly, Slide," the Story of Michael J. Kelly, the "King" of Baseball*, by Alfred P. Capio, a booklet published by the Passaic County Historical Society of New Jersey, 1962 (it has a bibliography of references); and "When Fans Roared 'Slide, Kelly, Slide!' at the Old Ball Game," by James A. Cox, in *The Smithsonian*, October 1982.

6. Nathaniel Frederick Pfeffer—"Unzer Fritz" the sports writers called him—was the star second baseman for the White Stockings in the 1880's. He was born in Louisville in 1860. A small paperback, *Scientific Ball*, which he wrote and published himself in 1889, is now much sought after by collectors.

One should not forget another well-known player on "Cap" Anson's team: outfielder Billy Sunday. Billy was a poor hitter, but fast on his feet and a clever base-stealer. Later he became the country's most famous soul-saver in the stretch of sinful years between the days of Dwight L. Moody and Billy Graham.

7. Fannin' bees: Tryout, or practice baseball games.

8. Poker dice: A game played with five dice, tossed from a cup. The object is to get the highest possible "hand," as in poker. The aces rank highest and are sometimes considered wild. Special dice are often used with card faces (from ace to nine) on the sides instead of spots.

8. HE NEVER HEARD OF CASEY!, by Grantland Rice

1. Cove: A slang word for "man," more common in England than here. It is comparable to "chap" or "bloke," but on what

The Oxford English Dictionary calls "a lower and more slangy stratum of speech." ("That old cove at the book-stall," wrote Dickens in *Oliver Twist*.)

2. Casey and his bat, but with subtle and probably intended overtones of Christ and the Cross.

3. *Wang has* been forgotten. One of Hopper's greatest stage triumphs was his starring role in *Wang*, a popular comic opera written in imitation of *The Mikado*, in which Hopper had previously starred. The play opened on Broadway in 1891, ran 151 performances, then went on tour in elegant railroad cars. A major logistic problem was the transportation of an elephant on which Wang, the regent of Siam, made his first stage entrance. "Wang goes with a bang!" read the advertisements.

The book was written by J. Cheever Goodwin, one of the most successful playwrights of the time. Though great financial successes, his plays have left less of an imprint on theatrical history than one ballad carelessly scribbled by Thayer. Woolson Morse wrote the music for *Wang*. Hopper was appearing in a revival of *Wang*, at Worcester, Massachusetts, when he met Thayer for the first time.

9. CASEY THE COMEBACK, by Herman J. Schiek

1. Look-in: Prospect of success.

10. WHY CASEY WHIFFED, by Don Fairbairn

1. Whiffed: See Note 2 of Grantland Rice's poem, *Mudville's Fate*.

2. Hoo-dooed: See Note 5 of the revised version of *Casey*.

11. CASEY AT THE PLATE, by W. B. France

1. The umpire was not Buttenheiser, who had called the famous third strike on Casey, but Herman "Squint" Jackson, a former Mudville pitcher. Jackson had left the team a few years before because of his failing eyesight.

12. THE COMING BACK OF CASEY, by Charles E. Jestings

1. On July 23, 1886, Steve Brodie jumped, or pretended to have jumped, off the Brooklyn Bridge. He was found in the water, but there were no witnesses. Assuming that Brodie did not fake

his jump, he committed the colossal blunder of not arranging to have his feat observed; hence "Brodie" came to mean any stupid mistake or blunder. The term is also used for the act of jumping from a high place to commit suicide.

2. The first names of these players and the positions they played remain unknown.

3. One away: One out.

4. Goose hung high: According to *The Macmillan Book of Proverbs, Maxims, & Famous Sayings,* page 1,010, the expression is believed to come from the older expression "the goose honks high." In fine weather geese fly high, hence the expression is a way of saying that fair weather is ahead and everything looks good.

5. Ready for the crate: Ready to be delivered.

13. THE MAN WHO FANNED CASEY, by "Sparkus"

1. Got on the chute: Slid down.

2. Since De Wolf Hopper first recited *Casey* in 1888, this suggests that *The Man Who Fanned Casey* was written in 1901 or later.

3. The lower floor of a theatre is called the parquet.

4. Mutt: See note 2 of "Casey—Twenty Years Later."

5. Frogtown: Centerville was situated on the western edge of Bugville Swamp, a region so heavily populated with bullfrogs that on quiet summer nights the frogs' croaking could actually be heard in Mudville, seven miles to the west. Nothing so infuriated a Centervillian as to hear a Mudvillian refer, as he usually did, to Centerville as "Frogtown."

6. Slabster: Pitcher. The "slab" is the pitcher's plate, hence "slabster," or, more commonly, "slabbist."

7. Sent balloonin': Sent up in the air, rattled.

8. Puff: Publicity plug.

9. Inshoot: A ball that curves toward the batter.

10. Pan: Plate.

11. An awkward way of saying that Fireball is planning another way to fool Casey.

12. Outshoot breaking wide: A ball curving out away from the batter.

13. Hangin' on the string: Hanging on the string of fate; a crucial moment.

14. The spitball, now prohibited, is a way of throwing a mighty curve by secretly applying spit to the ball.

14. CASEY ON A BAT, by William F. Kirk

1. The *Casey and the Bat* ballad runs to fifty-two stanzas which begin innocently enough:

> Things had been extra quiet at
> The Mudville Bar, that night;
> For there hadn't been an argument,
> And there hadn't been a fight.
>
> The boys were leaning on the bar,
> Having a drink or two,
> With nothing much to think about,
> And nothing much to do.

Then in walks "the damnedest bat in forty states," and things happen fast. Since a character in this ballad is named Pat Grogan (see the third line in the last stanza of Kirk's poem), one suspects that the Mudville Bar was somewhere near Boston, or the Boston team was somewhere near Mudville.

15. MRS. CASEY AT THE BAT, author unknown

1. Elizabeth Cooper, wife of the owner of Cooper's Grain and Feed Store, in Mudville. See *The Mighty Casey*, page 4.

2. Ethel Schmidt, niece of Homer Schmidt, Mudville's butcher. See *The Mighty Casey*, page 4.

3. Nellie O'Shaughnessy (in the opera *The Mighty Casey* she is called by her nickname "Merry") and Casey were married in October, 1887, a month after Casey's famous whiff. The ball park watchman, in the opera, recalls Nellie's skill in playing baseball when she was a little girl in pigtails. In this poem we observe her in action, six years after her marriage, as third baseman on the Mudville ladies' softball team.

4. Dorothy Flynn, wife of Roughhouse Flynn, Mudville's left fielder. See Note 6 on Thayer's original version of his ballad.

191

5. Not Emily Post but Henrietta Post, wife of Malcolm K. Post, founder and owner of Post's Nut and Bolt Manufacturing Company. Henrietta, known locally as the "Queen of Polecat Creek," was then the central figure in Centerville society.

16. CASEY'S SON, by Nitram Rendrag

1. Slamtown: A tiny village no longer on the map. It was then in Linn County, about fifteen miles northeast of Mudville.

2. Percy Dibble. His father was the Mudville veterinarian and homeopathic physician.

3. Donald Pringle, Mudville butcher.

4. Bingle: Common baseball slang for a single.

17. CASEY'S SISTER AT THE BAT, by James O'Dea

1. The position of catcher, the only player facing the sun.

2. Not girls from Vassar College, but from The Vassar Vinegar Works, in Bugville. The girls like to pretend (as indicated in the next line) that the company is their "varsity."

3. At the time this poem was written, "23" was still a popular all-purpose slang exclamation. See Note 3 of *Riley in the Box*.

18. CASEY'S DAUGHTER AT THE BAT, by Al Graham

1. Brenda Cooney: Daughter of Scooter Cooney, who had played shortstop with Casey. A right-hander, Brenda's nickname of "Lefty" derived from the fact that in the presidential campaigns of 1896 and 1900 she had helped her father distribute leaflets for William Jennings Bryan.

2. Barbara Barrows: Daughter of Otis Barrows, first baseman with Casey.

3. Myrna Flynn: Daughter of Roughhouse Flynn, left fielder on the old team with Casey.

4. Hedy ("Flatfoot") Blake: Daughter of James Elmer Blake, former Mudville third baseman. A vocalist with the Mudville Melodians, she was known in local musical circles as "Flatnote" Blake. In 1910 she married James Riley Snedeker, the pitcher who fanned Casey (see the introduction to *Riley in the Box*).

192

5. The umpire is Seymour Buttenheiser, from Bugville, whose father had umpired the historic game in which Casey struck out.

6. The pitcher for the Centervillettes is Wilma ("Sneaky") Snedeker, daughter of Fireball Snedeker, the Centerville pitcher who fanned Casey.

7. According to the *Dictionary of American Slang,* compiled by Harold Wentworth and Stuart Berg Flexner (Crowell, 1960), a "floogie" or "floogy" is "an average girl or young woman with a good but not beautiful face, an open honest personality, and a good spirit, but lacking in deep insight, good taste, refinement, and with no more and probably less than average intelligence." (*Cf.,* "The Flat-Foot Floogy with the Floy Floy," a popular song in 1945.) The word is now archaic. Not to be confused with "floosie," a promiscuous female.

8. A frump is a homely woman who wears dowdy, shabby, or old-fashioned clothes. The umpire is a man, but female epithets spring spontaneously from the lips of the enraged ladies in the bleachers.

19. CASEY'S DREAM, by William F. Robertson

1. Liner: A hard hit ball that travels almost in a straight line above the ground. Note that Casey is playing his usual position in the outfield.

2. Someone: Mrs. Casey, the former Nellie ("Merry") O'Shaughnessy. See Note 3 of *Mrs. Casey at the Bat.*

20. RILEY IN THE BOX, author unknown

1. Crackin' up: Praising. *Cf.,* the phrase, "It's not what it's cracked up to be."

2. Mutt: See Note 2 of *Casey—Twenty Years Later.*

3. The exclamation "Twenty-three skiddoo!", according to the *Dictionary of American Slang,* by Harold Wentworth and Stuart Berg Flexner (Crowell, 1960), was perhaps the "first truly national fad expression and one of the most popular fad expressions to appear in the U.S." Although now associated with the twenties, it actually flourished in the period from 1900 to 1910.

Pennants and arm bands were sold at resorts and county fairs bearing either "23" or "skiddoo" or both. The exclamation had no specific meaning: sometimes it expressed surprise or pleasure, sometimes displeasure or rejection. Here it obviously has the latter meaning.

21. CASEY ON THE MOUND, by Harry E. Jones

1. Bing Soph, Centerville's center fielder.

2. Bearcat: A powerful, aggressive ball player.

3. Tony Tittelbaum, formerly Tony Caesar, a big league umpire. Why Tony changed his name and left the big leagues for Kansas is told by Ogden Nash in his poem *Decline and Fall of a Roman Umpire*. The poem can be found in Nash's *Everyone But Thee and Me* (Little, Brown, 1957) and Lillian Morrison's anthology of sports poetry, *Sprints & Distances* (Crowell, 1965).

22. CASEY—TWENTY YEARS LATER, by Clarence P. McDonald

1. Bugville, in Linn County, Kansas, no longer exists, although it survived Mudville by some twenty years. It was a village at the southwestern edge of Bugville swamp, twelve miles southeast of Mudville and about eleven miles below Centerville.

2. At the time of this game the word "Mutt," a contraction of "mutton-head," meant a stupid, clumsy person. (*Cf.*, Mutt and Jeff.) Today the word refers only to a dog, especially a mongrel.

3. Dub: An inexperienced or poor player.

23. LIKE KELLY DID, by Clarence P. McDonald

1. The slide of Mike ("King") Kelly; see Note 5 of *The Man Who Played with Anson on the Old Chicago Team*.

2. Cops out the games: Wins the games.

3. Take a reef: Reduce your sails, go slower.

4. Heavy sticker: Top batter.

24. *CASEY—FORTY YEARS LATER,* by Neil McConlogue

1. Ballston Spa: A popular New York summer resort town about seven miles south of Saratoga Springs and famous for its medicinal spring water.

2. Pinchback suit: A man's suit with a coat that is cut or pleated to make it fit close to his back.

3. Midvale: A town (no longer existing) in Anderson County, Kansas, about ten miles south and west of Bugville. The terms "Acorns" and "Bears," for the Bugville and Midvale teams, did not become current until after World War I.

4. This is just one of old Casey's little jokes. At the time, "Doctor" John R. Brinkley, one of the nation's most successful quacks, was making a fortune by grafting goat glands to the testicles of aging men. Of course no goat gland was needed to provide virility for the Mighty Casey. He managed to keep himself in superb physical shape until his death on November 8, 1946, at the age of eighty-seven. He died in Topeka while visiting his oldest son Angus, who had settled there as founder and president of The Casey Suspenders Manufacturing Company.

26. *CASEY IN THE CAP,* by J. A. Lindon

1. Judging by these names, American cosmonauts are a terribly mixed-up crew.

2. A game played by children and nervous zoo-keepers. The Indian Rope Trick may have originated in snake-charmers shinning hastily up ladders that weren't there in order to escape from snakes that were.

3. This causes *capsulosis* or 'getting the lem,' a form of lunacy which is an occupational disease of cosmonauts. Symptoms include unusually rapid circulation, space-walking, flightiness, unearthly floating sensations, a tendency to moon around and the conviction that it is far better to go on working than to strike suddenly.

4. Lunar Excursion Module.

5. Ask any cop—if you've a thick skull.

27. *A VILLAGE CRICKET CASEY*, by J. A. Lindon

1. A stroke often played with nonchalance by those low down in the batting order, but never attempted by class batsmen, who simply haven't the technique for it. It is the cricketing equivalent of the bull's-eye scored by the big-game hunting tyro who, while aiming at a lion, neatly shoots dead the camel watching cautiously over his right shoulder, neither having noticed that the rifle was the wrong way round.

2. Two famous cricketers, very big fellows and identical twins, who played for the same county. (Or had I drunk a beer too many?)

3. The word 'duck' stands also, in cricket, for zero score (short for 'duck-egg,' from the shape). Both sorts of duck occur on the village green, but the cricketing variety rarely quack and waddle back to the pond.

4. The slight indentation a player makes with his bat in the turf (see stanza 7) so as to know when he is correctly positioned. Nothing to do with old-style executions.

28. *O'TOOLE'S TOUCHDOWN*, by Les Desmond

1. Hokus College, a small liberal arts school in Pokus, New Jersey.

2. Michael O'Toole, son of Red O'Toole who had been the catcher on Casey's team. Red was the nephew of Casey's mother. (See Note 1 of the first printing of *Casey at the Bat*.)

3. The University of Shemoken, in Shemoken, Wisconsin.

BIBLIOGRAPHY

PRINTINGS OF *CASEY*

The San Francisco Examiner, Sunday, June 3, 1888, p. 4, col. 4. This is the first printing.

New York Sporting Times, July 29, 1888. First reprinting that changed Casey to Kelly, Mudville to Boston.

Harvard University, Class of 1885: Secretary's Report No. V, 1900, pp. 88-90. Believed to be the first book printing of *Casey.*

Casey at the Bat. New Amsterdam Book Co., 1901. An anonymously illustrated booklet.

A Treasury of Humorous Poetry. Edited by Frederic Lawrence Knowles, Boston: 1902. First appearance of *Casey* in a hardcover anthology.

Casey at the Bat. New York: M. Witmark & Sons, 1904. Anonymously illustrated, eight-page booklet. Subtitled: Mr. De Wolf Hopper, the popular comic-opera comedian's version of the famous poem.

Casey at the Bat. Kansas City: H. G. Pert, 1905. An anonymously illustrated booklet. The text is stated to have been furnished by Thayer and approved by De Wolf Hopper.

The Bookman, Vol. 28, January, 1909, p. 434. Thayer's revised version.

Casey at the Bat. Chicago: A. C. McClurg and Co., 1912. A booklet illustrated by Dan Sayre Groesbeck.

The Home Book of Verse. Selected by Burton Egbert Stevenson. Henry Holt, 1912, pp. 2117-19. A corrupted version.

Sports Illustrated, April 9, 1956, p. 47. Illustrated by Marc Simont. Reprinted in *Children's Digest,* May, 1958, p. 98.

New York Sunday News, Coloroto Magazine, April 21, 1957. First printing of a two-page spread of *Casey,* lettered and illustrated in color by Steven R. Kidd. Reprinted April 5, 1959; April 16, 1961; April 12, 1964; April 10, 1966. Kidd's original painting now hangs in the National Baseball Museum, Cooperstown, N.Y.

Casey at the Bat. Illustrated by Jack Davis. *The Bedside Mad.* New American Library (Signet Books), 1959, pp. 140-57.

Casey at the Bat. Franklin Watts, 1964. Brief introduction by Casey Stengel, illustrations by Leonard Everett Fisher.

Casey at the Bat. Prentice-Hall, 1964. Illustrated by Paul Frame.

Casey at the Bat. Artist unidentified. *Children's Digest,* April 1967, pp. 17-24.

Casey at the Bat. Unidentified artist. *Echh,* a Marvel Comic book, August 9, 1968.

Casey at the Bat. Dover, 1977. Illustrated by Jim Hull, introduction by Martin Gardner.

Casey at the Bat. Coward, McCann & Geoghegan, 1978. Illustrated by Wallace Tripp.

ON ERNEST L. THAYER AND *CASEY*

Harvard University, Class of 1885: Secretary's Report No. IV, 1895. After the banquet, at the class reunion of 1895, Thayer gave an address and recited *Casey.* He is quoted in this earlier report, preceding the report in which his speech is recorded, as having written: "I will attempt to speak at our decennial dinner if I am not overcome by stage fright between now and then."

"Who Wrote 'Casey at the Bat'?" John W. Glenister. *Baseball Magazine,* Vol. 1, No. 2, June, 1908, pp. 59-60. The article presents several claimants, including Thayer, without taking sides.

"Casey at the Bat." Homer Croy. *Baseball Magazine,* Vol. 1, No. 6, October, 1908, pp. 10-12. An early interview with Thayer, mistaken in spots, but a valuable source.

"Who Wrote 'Casey at the Bat'?" Harry Thurston Peck. *The Scrap Book,* Vol. 6, December, 1908, pp. 947-54. An important article. It tells in detail the story of George Whitefield D'Vys' claim that he wrote *Casey,* refutes it, and establishes Thayer as the true author.

In spite of this thorough refutation, D'Vys' false claim lingered on for decades. *The New York Times,* as late as February 21, 1932, referred to it, prompting Thayer to write from California that "for this [*Casey*], perhaps the greatest of my sins, I was exclusively to blame." Thayer refers to Peck's 1908 article for a true account of the poem's history. Thayer's letter appeared in *The New York Times,* Sunday, March 13, 1932, Section III, page 2.

Through the generosity of Michael von Moschzisker, who reviewed the first edition of this book for *The Philadelphia Sunday Bulletin,* I came into the possession of a batch of material that had been sent to him by James A. Vance, a Philadelphian who had been a friend of D'Vys. The material included two printed booklets by D'Vys.

The larger booklet, *Cheering Some One On,* was printed in 1933 by C. A. A. Parker, Medford, Massachusetts. It contains 36 poems. One of them, *Casey's Confession,* is a reprinting of only the last two stanzas of a longer poem that appears in the other booklet, *"Casey at the Bat" and Other Mudville Ballads.* A photograph of D'Vys is on the cover. The printer is listed below as J. Frank Facey, 36 Prospect Street, Cambridge. There is no date.

The booklet contains eleven poems about Casey, the first being a corrupted version of Thayer's ballad. This is followed by *Casey's Confession.* Thayer's ballad is repeated, in slightly revised form, until Casey strikes out. Then come the final stanzas:

> "However did you do it?"
>   The fans still at me yell;
> So, I, to ease my mind a bit,
>   The secret now will tell.
> Just as the pitcher hurled the ball,
>   I saw, aback first base;
> The sweetest girl in Mudville
>   With happy beaming face.
>
> I knew that she was watching me,
>   I nerved to do my best;
> I swung my bat with fearful force
>   And—well you know the rest.
> But this I'll say in closing,
>   I'm sure beyond a doubt;
> Had I not eyed that pretty girl,
>   I wouldn't have struck out.

Casey in Reverse, the next ballad, tells in eight stanzas about a game in which Jim Casey—D'Vys always calls his Jim—is having bad luck batting right-handed. He switches to left, swats the first ball pitched, but absent-mindedly runs toward third instead of first. The poem ends:

> On, on, he sped! "Home run!" he glowed,
>   And not to be denied:
> Second and first he bounded o'er,
>   And came home with a slide.⁻
> "Git up!" roared Dolan, "You're a boob,
>   I hope you've tore your hide;
> For with that reverse stunt of yours,
>   One run's chopped off our side."
> And Mudville tears were shed o'er biers,
>   For half its fandom died.

I must say that this was such a good idea for a Casey poem that I am almost inclined to forgive D'Vys for his false claim.

Casey's "Phenom!", the next ballad, is a dull account of how Casey traded Flynn and Cooney for a young Dutch lad. When "Dutchy" strikes out in the final inning, the fans chase him off the field. *"Slide, Casey, Slide!"* is much funnier. The Dustville pitcher gives Jim Casey a walk, but instead of walking to first, Casey breaks into a run. He manages to round the bases, and after a goose-chase between third and home, he gets home safe with a mighty slide.

Casey in the Box has Casey pitching against Dustville. He is a great pitcher, but with one weakness—an inability to field bunts. The Dustville team knows this, but they hold off bunting until the last inning when three men bunt. Casey redeems himself by skillfully fielding all three balls and throwing the runners out.

In *Casey's Dream*, Jim finds himself welcomed to heaven by Saint Peter. When the soul of a former drinking companion comes up to him and whispers "Where can I get a drink?," Casey laughs so loud that he awakens his wife, who in turn wakes him. *At the Pipe* has D'Vys smoking his pipe and dreaming that he is a great player on Casey's team. *Mudville on the Map* praises the town, and urges that it be put on the map. *Casey's Jonah* reveals that Jim is an expert checker player. He is about to win a championship tournament when he is interrupted by his mother-in-law. She strides angrily into the room, a whip in hand, and orders him to go home and milk the cows.

Who Struck Billy Patterson? opens by likening the problem of Casey's authorship to an old riddle and a famous brain teaser by the American puzzle maker, Sam Loyd:

> There's "Who wrote Casey at the bat?"
>   The problem hard as sin;
> Because some seeking unearned crowns,
>   Have falsely butted in.
> "Why did the chicken cross that road?"
>   Has long been puzzling man;
> And there's another tough one, too,
>   'Tis this: "How old was Ann?"

Casey is dead, and attending the wake is a "temperance man" named Billy Patterson. He offends the mourners by refusing to drink. Someone puts out the lights, and in the dark Billy is badly beaten up. A policeman who arrives on the scene stops wondering who wrote *Casey,* and asks "Who struck Bill Patterson?" The ballad concludes: "I cannot tell, can you?" Was D'Vys thinking, perhaps unconsciously, of his own inability to answer truthfully the question of who wrote *Casey?*

The last ballad, *Casey up Aloft,* has pasted over it a revised version clipped from a newspaper. The scene is Joyland, on a distant planet where a ball team from Saturn is playing a team from Mars. The Saturn team consists of Lefty Grove (pitcher); Cochrane (catcher); Gehrig, Traynor, Ty Cobb, and Maranville on the infield; Al Simmons, Pepper Martin, and Babe Ruth in the outfield. The Mars team is made up of Casey and his Mudville teammates. Casey wins the game with a "mighty swat" that sends the "apple whizzing" while ten million fans cheer.

Both books are inscribed by D'Vys to his friend Vance, and accompanying them are four typed letters from D'Vys to Vance, written in 1933 and 1934. D'Vys wrote from The Cambridge Home for the Aged, where he was recovering from severe injuries acquired when he was struck by a car. They are sad letters. In one letter, D'Vys thanks his friend for telling him that his (Vance's) father had always believed that D'Vys was the real author of *Casey*. He adds that he knows of at least fourteen claimants, citing Thayer as the most "unyielding" of them all. A second letter complains that he is being "attacked" by De Wolf Hopper, who has "netted a goodly harvest of coins . . . by reciting my brain child." Apparently D'Vys had asked Hopper for money, and Hopper had angrily refused. In another letter he speaks proudly of a daughter and grandson, and mentions the manuscript of his unpublished novel, *Everybody's Goat*.

The letters are the rambling, disconnected thoughts of a sick old man, almost totally blind, still clinging to the conviction—which he may now actually believe—that he wrote *Casey*. In one letter he even speaks of hearing "a few months ago" from a priest who said he had come upon a copy of *The Sporting Times*, dated August 14, 1886, that contained *Casey*, signed "Anonymous, Somerville, Mass." I do not know when D'Vys died, but he surely died without altering his claim.

America's National Game. Albert G. Spaulding. American Sports Publishing Co., 1911. Chapter thirty-two tells the poem's story, includes a drawing of Thayer.

Famous Single Poems. Burton Egbert Stevenson. Harcourt, Brace and Co., 1923. Revised edition, Dodd, Mead and Co., 1935. The chapter on *Casey* originally appeared in the *New York Herald*, January 14, 1923, page 7.

"Casey at the Bat." De Wolf Hopper and Wesley Winans Stout. *Saturday Evening Post*, Vol. 198, No. 20, November 14, 1925. p. 8f. Reprinted as Chapter 3 of Hopper's autobiography (written in collaboration with Stout), *Once a Clown Always a Clown*, Little, Brown and Co., 1927.

Santa Barbara News-Press, August 22, 1940. Informative obituary on Thayer.

The National Cyclopedia of American Biography, Vol. 33, 1947, p. 104. Biography of Thayer, with excellent photograph.

Horatius at the Bridge and Casey at the Bat. Arthur Leonard Bloomfield. Privately printed by the Grabhorn Press, San Francisco, 1954. Edition limited to seventy-five copies.

This is a large, folded sheet of four pages on which Bloomfield argues that Casey is an intended satire on Thomas Babbington Macaulay's much longer ballad, *Horatius at the Bridge*. In addition to having a similar metrical form, Bloomfield points out that: "Both pieces deal with a supreme crisis in which all depends on a 'superman' 'coming-through.' In both, a large crowd looks on impotent to act and with all the tragic implications of such a situation. Horatius succeeds, to be sure, while Casey fails; but Casey's failure is of no less epic proportions. . . . Finally, after the supreme crisis, both ballads pass into a serene and almost wistful mood. . . . We conclude therefore that *Casey at the Bat,* far from being of the Brooklyn bleachers, emanates from the study of a clever satirist. Thayer probably hated memorizing *Horatius* in prep-school, and how he must have enjoyed taking it out on Casey!"

Bloomfield prints six stanzas from each ballad, in parallel columns, to point up what he considers similarities in style and tone; but the parallels are weak. Thayer may have consciously or unconsciously thought of *Horatius* when he wrote *Casey,* but one is inclined to agree with Burton Stevenson who considered the question briefly in his *Famous Single Poems,* listed above. "*Casey at the Bat* in no way suggests *Horatius,*" Stevenson wrote, "except perhaps by a very faint similarity in the basic idea. But its form and character are entirely different . . ."

The Mighty Casey. G. Schirmer, Inc., 1954. (Obtainable postpaid from the publishers, 3 E. 43rd St., New York, New York 10017.) This is the libretto and complete vocal score of the opera by William Schuman and Jeremy Gury. The paperback cover reproduces a painting by the late Albert Dorne (he died in 1965), the well-known illustrator who founded the Famous Artists School for teaching art by mail. The painting, showing Casey completing his fatal swing, was originally done for the John Hancock Mutual Life Insurance Company as one of a series of illustrations of "Great Americans" that have appeared in magazine advertisements since 1947. The Casey ad ran in *Life, The Saturday Evening Post,* and other mass-circulation magazines in 1949. The original painting is now owned by Joe Cronin, president of the American League.

The Hot Stove League. Lee Allen. A. S. Barnes, 1955. Chapter 20, "No Joy in Mudville," tells the story of the ballad, reprints Thayer's newspaper letter in which he denies that Casey is based on any actual ball player.

"Seventy-Five Years Ago." Anthony Austin. *New York Times Magazine,* June 9, 1963, p. 51f. A short piece on the history of *Casey.* Reproduces an illustration from the 1901 booklet.

"The Harvard Man Who Put the Ease in Casey's Manner." Martin Gardner. *Sports Illustrated,* Vol. 22, No. 21, May 24, 1965, eastern edition, pp. E5-E8 (western edition, June 28; midwestern edition, August 2). Reprinted, with revisions and additions, at the beginning of this book.

APPENDIX I

THAYER'S OTHER BALLADS

No definitive check list is available for other ballads and humorous poems by Thayer that were published in the *San Francisco Examiner* in 1887 and 1888, or in the *New York Journal* in 1896. In one harried afternoon at the Library of Congress, turning crumbling pages, I found the following six ballads in the *Examiner*.

A Ballad: The strange story of a highly educated young lady (October 2, 1887, p. 9; eighteen stanzas of four lines each). Mehitabel Caist is in love with two men, one of "scholarly bent," the other of "muscle and brawn." She solves her problem by marrying neither. When she feels like talking, or being escorted to a party, she calls on her "muscleless Homer"—

> While Jimmy Laertius Hind
>   Coming two or three times in a week,
> In privacy squeezed her, and secretly pleased her,
>   By rubbing his nose on her cheek.

A Ballad: A medieval pa who disregarded the customs of his time (October 16, 1887, p. 9; ten stanzas of eight lines each). A knight rescues a beautiful lady who had been locked in a dungeon by her father, only to discover (after slaying the father) that the poor girl is insane.

A Ballad: The shocking tale of an extremely accomplished villain (October 23, 1887, p. 9; eighteen stanzas of four lines each). Jonathan Depew, a gentleman skilled in the art of flattery, meets with just retribution after he makes the mistake of telling each of two sisters that the other sister is beautiful:

> The time is twelve o'clock about, the scene a narrow street;
> A cry of murder rouses a policeman on his beat;
> He rushes to the rescue and discovers with a start
> Mr. Jonathan Depew with two (2) daggers in his heart.

A Ballad: The marvelous cure operated by the famous Dr. Twist (November 6, 1887, p. 10; twenty-four stanzas of four lines each). When Jane Gray's lover, Private May, goes off to war, the heartbroken girl refuses to eat. She becomes so thin that her father calls on the services of Dr. Twist, a famous homeopathic physician. (On homeopathy, see my *Fads and Fallacies,* a Dover paperback, Chapter 16.) Dr. Twist diagnoses the girl's symptoms as caused by love; so, applying the homeopathic principle of *similia similibus curantur* (like cures like), he proceeds to make his own amorous advances:

> Poor love-sick Jane could not resist
> The remedies of Dr. Twist;
> Day after day she showed a fresh
> And noticeable gain in flesh.
>
> On Monday she regained her legs,
> And Tuesday called for ham and eggs,
> And Wednesday Dr. Twist assured
> Her parents that the child was cured.
>
> Then Dr. Twist, as doctors will,
> Put in his little doctor's bill,
> Amounting to a total which
> Assumed that Jane's papa was rich.
>
> He charged for kisses, flowers and hugs,
> Entitling them "erotic drugs."
> He also charged enormously
> For writing bits of poetry.

Mr. Gray goes broke paying the bill. Private May returns, but after learning about the financial plight of Jane's father, decides not to marry her.

A Ballad: The strange romance of a bold but unfortunate detective (November 20, 1887, p. 9; twenty-two stanzas of four lines each). A detective is so skilled in the art of disguise that he becomes an entirely different personality each time he plays a new role. The only trait common to all his personalities is a liking for cake, especially the cake served at a certain coffee house:

> And this hankering for cake, sir, plus a tenderness for smelts,
> Is my only means of knowing that I ain't somebody else.

Playing the role of Peter, he falls in love with Lizzie Fay, the coffee-house waitress. Later, as a new character named Billy, he goes to the same coffee house where he again falls in love with Lizzie. Still later, when he is back in his Peter disguise, Lizzie refuses to see him because her heart is now with Billy:

> And, as Peter, I experienced a strong desire to kill
> The man who had deceived me in the character of Bill;
> And it's even more than likely that to kill him I'd have tried,
> If I hadn't had a horror of committing suicide.

In his agony, the detective cracks up, but he recovers, as Peter, to tell his sad tale.

A Sea Ballad: Thrilling account of an incident in American daily life (December 4, 1887, p. 13; twenty-three stanzas of four lines each). This, apparently, was the last ballad written by Thayer before an illness forced him to return to his home in Worcester. It is here reprinted in its entirety.

A SEA BALLAD

Thrilling Account of an Incident in American Navy Life

THE HEROIC CAPTAIN.

Something Which Will Make the Hearts of American Citizens Glow With Pride.

The author of this little ballad has long and ardently desired to immortalize in song an American naval officer of the present generation, but as the dove of peace seems to have permanently roosted on this country, and as the events of the last few years

have yielded no material for sea verse of an heroic nature, the
author is fain to content himself with a fictitious but not altogether improbable incident. He does not expect that his little
yarn will immortalize anybody.

Oh, list to the moan of a toothless gale,
  Of a gale too weak to roar,
And hark to the swash of the waves that wash
  A pleasant, sandy shore.

For I sing a song of a captain bold,
  More bold than tongue can tell—
Much bolder than he whose name we see
  In the yarn of the Nancy Bell.

I am sure my hero was very brave,
  And a trifle reckless, for
The venturesome man he sailed in an
  American man-of-war.

And he took his ship many miles from land
  Where the water is deep and cold;
All honor to him, for he couldn't swim,
  Could not this Captain bold.

He could saw a board and stop a leak,
  And mend anything that broke;
He could patch a sail and drive a nail,
  But he couldn't swim a stroke.

The Admiral summoned this Captain once,
  And he gravely said to him,
"I admire your sand, but I must demand
  Of you to learn to swim.

"It's all well enough to show the stuff
  Of which a Captain's made,
And I much approve of the courage you've
  So frequently displayed;

"But we must consider this subject from
  A patriot's point of view:
Suppose you drown when the ship goes down,
  Then who'll command the crew?"

The brow of the Captain bold grew stern,
  And he drew a labored breath,
And he dashed his eyes if he'd jeopardize
  His show for a gallant death.

"If I learn to swim," the Captain said,
  "What prospect could there be
For me to win any glory in
  The United States navee?"

The Admiral thought for a while, and then
  He cried: "If the ship goes down,
To hell with the crew; a man like you
  Mustn't lose a chance to drown."

Well, the Captain put to sea next day,
  And his heart was blithesome when
He found by the lead it was over his head,
  But that didn't please his men.

That night it blew a downright breeze,
  The waves ran toad-stools high,
And above the shrouds a number of clouds
  Were clear to the naked eye.

The Captain stood on the forward deck,
  And he trembled for his craft;
He knew it must be a dangerous sea,
  For he plainly felt the draft.

And the heart of the Captain bold grew faint,
  And pale grew the Captain's cheek,
When he heard that cry so dreaded by
  All men-of-war's men, "a leak."

Then the boatswain piped all hands on deck,
  And the carpenter took command,
And in order to encourage the crew
  The chaplain prayed for land.

They manned their togs, those sad sea-dogs,
  And they stood by the cold roast pig,
But there wasn't enough loose matter to stuff
  Up the hole—it was so big.

So the carpenter came to the Captain bold,
    And he mildly said to him:
"You'll surely drown when the ship goes down,
    For you don't know how to swim.

"We've done our best to fill that hole,
    But the ship is bound to sink,
Unless you are willing to serve us as filling,
    Which is little to ask, I think."

The Captain greeted this speech with joy,
    And the carpenter's hand he seized,
And he tried as well as he could to tell
    How deeply he'd be pleased.

The carpenter wept. "How kind," he said.
    "Not at all," said the Captain bold.
Then he clapped, did the "Cap," himself in
        the gap
    In the side of the good ship's hold.

He stopped that hole head first, he did
    And a bubble rose on the sea,
And when it broke that bubble it spoke,
    And it said, "Hooray for me!"

And that was the end of the Captain bold,
    And it's just as well that he died,
For the very next day his ship, they say,
    Was wrecked by the rising tide.

Oh, list to the moan of a toothless gale,
    Of a gale too weak to roar,
And hark to the swash of the waves that wash
    A pleasant, sandy shore.

All six of these ballads were given prominent heads and sub-heads, at the top of a page, and were illustrated throughout with small cartoons. It is interesting to note that, in contrast, *Casey at the Bat* (which Thayer mailed to the paper from his home in Massachusetts) was buried in the middle of an editorial page, Sunday, June 3, 1888, with a tiny heading and no illustrations. Thayer always maintained that it was no better or worse than his other ballads, but of course he was mistaken.

In the fall and winter of 1896, possibly on into 1897, Thayer contributed four or five ballads to *The American Humorist*, the Sunday supplement of Hearst's *New York Journal*. Like his earlier ballads, they struck notes of tragic, at times sadistic, comedy. Thayer told Homer Croy (see bibliography) that the best of these was about a New York City politician and called *Murphy's Pig*, but I was unable to find a ballad of this title; nor could I locate *Oppenheimer's Barbecue* which Burton Stevenson says appeared in the *Journal* also during this period, but not in the supplement. The three I found are:

The Very Moving Ballad of Ross McCann (November 1, 1896, p. 6; twenty-two stanzas of four lines each). Ross is a gentle fellow who is so easily offended by off-color remarks that he reads nothing but chidren's books and an expurgated Bible. A man who enjoys dirty jokes has Ross bashed on the head by two hirelings, takes him captive, and forces him to listen to bawdy stories and songs until the poor man goes out of his skull and dies.

> Henceforth on angel wings he'll skim
> Through heaven's unmeasured reach;
> Let's hope the saints who skim with him
> Are guarded in their speech.

Malony's Wife (November 29, 1896, p. 3; four stanzas of eight lines each). Malony's wife is virtuous, with a heart of gold, but she has a flirtatious glint in her eye that drives men wild:

> The boys do kiss Malony's wife;
> And it's wrong.
> But you can't resist her to save your life
> For long.
> You ought not to do what it's wrong to do,
> But you look at her and she looks at you,
> And then you commit Malony to
> Hong Kong.

Clancy Pays the Bill (December 6, 1896, p. 6; thirteen stanzas of four lines each). Two young Irish lads treat themselves to an expensive dinner at a French restaurant, only to discover that they lack sufficient money to pay the bill. Clancy, a lonely old Irishman who has been sitting at the next table, comes to their rescue, and adds that it would be an honor to sup with them sometime. So every Tuesday night, thereafter, the two men dine with the stupid, but kindly and wealthy, Mr. Clancy, who always picks up the tab:

> And when conversation languishes we fill a glass and yell:
> "How are you, Mr. Clancy?" and he answers "Oi am well."

In searching for these and the earlier ballads I did not have time to check daily papers, but in turning the brittle pages my eyes caught a short poem called "Music by the Band" (it recommended voting for Cleveland), in a Monday edition of the *San Francisco Examiner*, July 9, 1888, p. 4, col. 3. It was signed "Phin," so there may have been a number of short poems by Thayer, as well as much of his unsigned prose material, in the *Examiner's* weekday editions.

POSTSCRIPT

The two ballads I tried unsuccessfully to run down, *Murphy's Pig* and *Oppenheimer's Barbecue,* proved to be one and the same. Jim Lyons, of Mountain View, California, sent me a copy of this 18-stanza ballad as it appeared in *The San Francisco Examiner*, November 8, 1896, under the title *Oppenheimer's Barbecue*. It has the dubious triple distinction of being anti-Irish, anti-Jewish, and anti-black. The ballad tells about a big-city political boss named Murphy, and his enemy, Moses Oppenheimer, who seeks to replace him in a coming election. Moses throws a free barbecue party for the Jewish voters of the district, but Murphy's pig accidentally falls into the barbecue pit. When the "nigger" cook sticks his fork into what he thinks is roast ox, he comes up with the dying pig. The guests are horrified, and Moses, having struck out like Casey, is forced to leave town. I quote the final stanza:

> Garland-laden every May Day,
>   Where the pig weed spreads its bloom,
> Be it bright or be it gray day,
>   Murphy weeps beside a tomb.
> There a martyr's name is cherished
>   With what fervor love can give;
> Here reposeth one who perished
>   That the government might live.

Lyons also discovered two Thayer poems that appeared in the same newspaper on August 5, 1888, two months after *Casey*. A 19-stanza ballad, *Editha's Shame: The Pardonable Greed of a Young Lady from the Country,* is on page 9. Editha Belle Ballou is a wealthy young lady who wants to be even wealthier. One day, when she is walking alone in a field, a rude stranger grabs and kisses her. Editha takes him to court. She asks for fifty thousand dollars, but the jury allows her only ten thousand. The poem ends:

> So never will Editha's eyes
>   Be free from bitter tears again,
> For on her maiden soul there lies
>   A forty-thousand-dollar stain.
>
> In undefiled virginity,
>   In uncontaminated thought,
> In perfect girlish goodness she
>   Is forty thousand dollars short.

In the same issue, page 4, is a short political poem by Thayer, *Ben Serenades the Working Class.* Ben is Benjamin Harrison, who became the twenty-third president of the United States. In the poem, he pleads for the support of the working classes, for whom he has developed a sudden love since he became the Republican candidate in June.

APPENDIX II

MORE SEQUELS AND PARODIES

Since the first edition of this book was published, many new parodies and sequels to Casey have been written, and older ones have been discovered. When readers started sending them, I had hopes of adding a few of the better ones to a new edition. Alas, there are far too many, so I must content myself with brief descriptions.

Mad magazine periodically prints parodies of *Casey* written by Frank Jacobs, a Manhattan writer who is *Mad*'s most prolific contributor (more than 400 pieces, not to mention his eleven original *Mad* paperbacks). His *Casey at the Dice* begins: "The table wasn't breaking for the Vegas crowd that night". Epstein rolls snake-eyes, and when Spinelli misses his point, a mood of deep depression settles over the players. If only Casey would arrive to roll the bones!

> Then, suddenly, their eyes lit up;
>   A cry rose from their lips;
> It echoed off the slot machines,
>   It rattled off the chips;
>
> It rumbled through the Black Jack games
>   While cards were being dealt;
> For Casey, lucky Casey,
>   Was advancing to the felt!

With nails cleanly manicured, his face tan, sporting an iridescent silk suit and ruby cufflinks, Casey coolly places his bet. The others bet with him. A hush falls at the table as Casey blows on the dice and raises his arm. "And now the air is shattered by the force of Casey's throw!"

> Oh, somewhere in this wealthy land
>   There is a happy spot
> Where naturals are being rolled
>   And dice are running hot;
>
> And somewhere men are doubling up
>   And winners scream and shout;
> But there is no joy in Vegas—
>   Lucky Casey has crapped out!
>
> © 1968 by E. C. Publications, Inc.

Jacobs's *Howard at the Mike* (December 1972; reprinted in *The Abominable Snow Mad*) tells how the television fans grow bored by the football game they are watching because Howard Cosell, suffering from a bad cold, is not there to narrate the game. Early in the second half, a mighty cheer goes up in the broadcast booth. The great Howard is advancing toward the mike. Here are the tragic final stanzas:

> A glint has come to Howard's eyes, his tongue is poised to strike;
> His hand is raised to make a point, he leans into his mike;
> And now we feel the fury of that mighty mind of his—
> And now the air is shattered as he tells it like it is.
>
> Oh, somewhere in this favored land there is a happy place
> Where folks are watching re-runs of "I Spy" and "Lost in Space";
> And somewhere there are TV sets around which folks rejoice;
> But there is no joy in football—gabby Howard's lost his voice.
>
> © 1972 by E. C. Publications, Inc.

The September 1977 *Mad* contained *Casey at the Talks,* another parody by the incomparable Jacobs. The owners of the Mudville team are in deep gloom because they have been unable to sign up Casey for the coming season. In strides mighty Casey, accompanied by two lawyers, three accountants, and his business agent. "The owners lauded Casey's clothes, extolled his wavy hair; they kissed the leather of his shoes and knelt beside his chair." Casey is offered a million bucks, plus ten percent of grandstand sales, shares of stock, a butler, and a custom-built Rolls Royce.

> The smile is gone from Casey's lips, his countenance is stern;
> He grips his chair with knuckles white, he gives his head a turn;
> And now he flicks an eyebrow at his agent standing by,
> And now the air is shattered by the words of his reply.
>
> Oh, somewhere in the baseball world there is a happy town,
> Where management has signed a star who'll win the triple crown;

And somewhere fans stand up to cheer a bases-loaded clout,
But there is no joy in Mudville—Mighty Casey has held out.

> © 1977 by E. C. Publications, Inc.

The Mad Jock Book (1983), written by Jacobs and illustrated by Jack Davis, has still another parody, *Casey at the Hoop*. Casey is the seven-foot star player of the Mudville basketball team who has been out of the game because of a virus. Mudville is losing, but Casey shows up and enters the game when there is one second remaining.

Oh, somewhere in this happy land the parties have begun,
And somewhere people jump with joy as championships are won,
And somewhere you can hear a "swish" as balls are cleanly sunk,
But there is no joy in Mudville—Mighty Casey missed the dunk.

> © 1983 by Frank Jacobs and E. C. Publications, Inc.

Jacobs's version of Thayer's ballad as it might have been written by Edgar Allen Poe ("Once upon a final inning, with the other ball-team winning, and my Mudville teammates trailing by a score of 2 to 4 . . ." appeared in *Mad*, March 1963, along with Jacobs's version of *The Midnight Ride of Paul Revere* as it might have been written by Thayer. (Both poems were reprinted in *Mad Special*, Book 9.) The second poem ends:

Oh, somewhere in this war-torn land the people safely know
That Redcoats are invading, taking captives as they go;
And somewhere people are prepared to flee the British force,
But there's no hope for New England—
Paul Revere can't ride a horse!

> © 1962 by E. C. Publications, Inc.

Art Buchwald is responsible for eleven stanzas about how Casey tried to take advantage of the new ruling that allows women reporters in baseball locker rooms. Cooney and Barrows fail to impress the gorgeous lady reporter who invades the locker room to find out why Mudville lost the game. Casey tries to score but gets nowhere on his first two passes. He makes a third attempt, but she socks his ear and kicks his shin. The ballad first appeared in Buchwald's newspaper column (October 8, 1978), and is reprinted in his book *Laid Back in Washington* (1981).

The New York Times (December 11, 1948) published an excellent political parody of *Casey* by Lee W. O'Brien, an INS correspondent who recited it at a political rally in Albany, New York, on December 10. It begins:

It looked extremely doubtful for the Democrats last June;
The South was in rebellion, the Wallace boom in bloom.

214

And so when General Ike said "No," and Douglas did the same,
They sadly turned to Harry, and Harry he was game.

Twelve more stanzas tell the story of the 1948 presidential election when all the polls predicted an easy victory for Thomas Dewey. The ballad ends: "And somewhere men are laughing, and somewhere children shout, but there is no joy in GOP—Harry Truman struck 'em out."

Cathy at the Bat, by Tom Koch, appeared in *Mad* in July 1979. Mudville fans are shocked when the team allows Cathy to play in a game. They expect the worst, but shapely Cathy surprises them by slamming the winning home run.

New York City's Mayor John Lindsay tried his hand at parodying *Casey*. His four-stanza *Ode to the New York Mets* ran in *The New York Times* (October 10, 1969). It predicted that the New York Mets would trounce the Baltimore Orioles in the coming World Series. The Mets did not strike out, but won the series 4 to 1. The following year saw the publication of *Joy in Mudville,* George Vecsey's history of the Mets.

4F Casey at the Bat was sent to me by Clifford C. Merkle, of Scotia, New York. He thinks it appeared in the *Baltimore Sun* near the end of World War II, and that Grantland Rice was the author, but he isn't sure. It is a sixteen-stanza ballad about an aging Casey. The war draft has taken Cooney and Barrows, but Casey has been declared 4F, so he is still playing for Mudville. Arthritis makes him limp to the plate. When he doffs his cap, dandruff blows into the umpire's eyes. His teeth drop out, he loses a glass eye, and he is too deaf to hear what the umpire shouts. On the final pitch, Casey drops his bat and slams the ball with his wooden leg. It is a home run, but Casey has to round the bases in a wheelchair.

Oh, somewhere folks are wearyin', and somewhere there is gloom,
And somewhere cruel despots lead whole nations to their doom.
But Mudville, once so joyless, is as sunny as Siam,
Since Casey socked that homer with his bird's-eye maple gam.

Robert C. Landes, of Columbus, Ohio, sent me a copy of his unpublished *Casey Playing Left*. Mudville leads 4 to 1, it is the final inning, and the opposing team has the bases loaded. Casey is summoned to play left field. Casey grabs the ball when it bounces off the fence, "and now the air is shattered by the force of Casey's throw." The last sad couplet is:

But men laugh not in Mudville, and children's shouts are few,
For no one ever found the ball that mighty Casey threw.

Dick Kaegel, associate editor of *The Sporting News,* found two Casey ballads in a book titled *Pep: The Red Book of Sports for Red-Blooded Readers.* The book has no date or publisher, but Kaegel guesses it was printed about 1920 by the *Pittsburgh Gazette Times.* It is a book of sports poems by the newspaper's reporter George S. Applegarth, who used the byline "Appy." *The Man Who Struck Out Casey* (eighteen stanzas) is a retelling of the game by Jackie Wienerkraut, the pitcher. *Why Casey Fanned,* in eleven stanzas, reveals that Wienerkraut had a glass eye. Just before Casey's final swing, he used the eye to blind Casey with a beam of reflected sunlight.

Kaegel also sent an unpublished *Casey's Son* that had been submitted to *The Sporting News* by Richard Knudsen, of Spencer, Iowa, and a copy of *The Congressional Record* (February 16, 1947) that reprints *Riley in the Box,* by James Patrick McGovern. This ballad had been recited to a session of Congress by Arizona representative Richard F. Harless, who said it had appeared in *The Arizona Daily Sun* (January 29, 1947). The poem's eight stanzas, like the ballad of the same name that I reprinted, is a tribute to the pitcher who struck Casey out.

Another tribute to Riley, titled *Riley on the Mound,* was written by the "lovable lush," comedian Foster Brooks. Brooks recited the poem in strong Irish brogue on several television shows, including the Johnny Carson show in 1974. It was recorded and issued in 1978 by Horizon Records, Box 32, Minersville, Pennsylvania, in a folder that prints the twenty-two stanzas alongside Thayer's original ballad.

W. W. Denslow, the first illustrator of *The Wizard of Oz,* has the following quatrain in his book for children, *When I Grow Up* (Century Company, 1909):

> When I grow up and am as big
>   As "Casey at the Bat,"
> They'll not catch *me* with "one! two! three!"
>   *I'll* not strike out like that!

One of Denslow's drawings is a caricature of De Wolf Hopper posing on home plate as Casey.

Someone sent me a magazine tearsheet (no indication of its date or source) that is a full-page advertisement for Talon's nylon Zephyr zipper. Under a drawing of Casey swinging his bat is the following quatrain:

> They didn't know that day in Mudville
>   Whether to laugh or cry.

> For as Mighty Casey swung and missed,
> He also popped his fly.

Russell Baker's column in *The New York Times* (April 9, 1977) is headed "Out at the New Ball Game." It is an amusing prose account of the game in which Casey fanned, told as Ring Lardner might have written it if the game had been played today.

At least one science fiction story has been based on Thayer's ballad. Titled "Joy in Mudville," by Poul Anderson and Gordon W. Dickson, it first appeared in *Fantasy and Science Fiction* in 1955, and was reprinted in *The Infinite Arena: Seven Science Fiction Stories About Sports* (1977), edited by Terry Carr. I wouldn't have known of it had not Ronald C. Semone, of Washington, D.C., sent me a copy.

It is a wild tale. On the planet Toka, the native Hokas have assimilated Earth culture so thoroughly that their national sport is baseball. Casey, their star player, actually believes he is the legendary Casey of Thayer's ballad. In a crucial ball game against the reptilian Sarennians, when Casey is at bat in the last inning, the sneaky Sarennians wheel a public address system out of their dugout to blare forth a tape recording of *Casey at the Bat.*

Casey is so mortified by this reminder of his big failure that he falls to the ground, sobbing and pawing the dirt. He is urged to get up, but he can't. "Muh heart ain't in it no more," he cries. "Dey trusted me in Mudville and I let 'em down." The recording continues to the end. Casey and his team are totally demoralized.

The game is saved when Alexander Jones, a Hoka poet, seizes the microphone and improvises the following stanzas:

> But hold, what strikes the umpire, what causes him to glare
>   With fiery look and awful eye upon the pitcher there?
> And Casey takes the catcher by the collar with his hand;
>   He hales him to the umpire and together there they stand.
>
> "I bid you look," cried Casey. "I bid you search him well.
>   For such as these our fine fair game they soon would sound its knell—"
> The umpire checks them over and the villains' faces fall
>   When out from each one's pocket he pulls forth *a hidden ball!*
>
> "Oh, shame!" cries out the Mudville crowd. The echoes answer "Shame!"
>   "That such a dirty low-down trick should blight our Casey's name.
> The pitcher only faked his throw, the catcher faked his catch.
>   The cowards knew that such as they were never Casey's match."

"Now take your places once again. Once more!" the umpire
cried.
   "And your next pitches will be fair or else I'll have your hide.
Now take your places once again, to places one and all!"
   And as soon as they were ready, the umpire cried, "Play ball!"

And now the pitcher takes his stance, his face is black and grim,
   And he starts his furious windup with a fearful verve and vim.
And now he rocks back on his heel; and now he lets it fly.
   The ball comes sizzling forward watched by Casey's steely eye.

For Casey does not tremble, mighty Casey does not balk,
   Though it's clear the ball is high and wide, and they aim to
      make him walk.
He steps forward in the batter's box, his bat's a lambent flame.
   Crack! Smash! The ball flies o'er the fence—*and Casey wins
      the game!*

As Jones recites the surprise ending, Casey's confidence returns,
and he slams a homer over left field. The Hokas have won the
Sector pennant, making them eligible to compete in the Galactic
Series.

For the record, here are some more Casey ballads that have
come to my attention:

Casey's Revenge, by Chesley Poore, *Baseball Magazine* (September 1935, page 440). Casey is so pleased when he finally hits a
homer that he runs around the bases twice.

When Casey Slugged the Ball, by Nat Wright, *Sporting News*
(November 11, 1899, page 6). After redeeming himself in a game,
Casey becomes mayor of Mudville and the town is renamed
Caseyville.

Casey as an Umpire, by Henry P. McFarland, *Sporting Life*
(June 6, 1968, page 6). This short poem appeals to Casey to settle
once and for all who wrote the original ballad, Ernest Thayer or
George D'Vys.

Casey as a Fan, by Russell Askue, *Baseball Magazine,* date unknown. His playing days over, Casey becomes a loyal Yankee fan.

Casey's Son, by Ferguson Fague, *Baseball Magazine* (January
1911, pages 61-62). In a crucial game with Slamtown, the son bats
in the wining run.

Casey Comes Back, by Oswald N. Burke, *Baseball Magazine*
(October 1929, page 510). Casey wins a game with a homer.

Rudi at the Met, anonymous, *National Lampoon* (May 1972,
page 64). The ballad describes a series of mishaps during a ballet in
which Rudi is the star dancer.

1941: Casey in the Box, by Meyer Berger, in *The Second Fireside Book of Baseball* (1958), edited by Charles Eisenstein. The poor pitching of Hugh Casey loses a game for the Brooklyn Dodgers.

Modern Casey at the Bat, by H. I. Phillips, in *The Sporting News* (June 26, 1946), apparently reprinted from Phillips's column in *The New York Sun.* This is a satire on labor unions and politicians. When a second strike is called on Casey, his teammates cry "Fraud!" a fact-finding board goes into session, politicians make speeches, President Truman is awed, and Casey, instead of striking out, finally walks out.

Casey at the Bridge Table, by Shepard Barclay, in his book *Bridge Fun: Verse and Worse* (1934). Casey fails to make a slam in a bridge contest between Mudville and Slamtown.

Yamashita at the Bat. Ronald C. Semone writes that in the early fifties he heard a 45-recording of this retelling of the Casey legend in Japanese broken English, containing such lines as "So solly, honorable umpire is blind as a bat." Does anyone know more about this?

Manuel Penner, of New York City, recalls a Casey ballad that he heard during World War II years. It has me intrigued, but I have not been successful in running it down. Penner recalls the opening line as: "Now Casey's gone to Kingdom come, where all good players go." When Casey is taken to Saint Peter, he starts to recite Thayer's poem. Penner says the final stanza went something like this:

> "The outlook wasn't brilliant"—that's as far as Casey got,
>   When Peter grabbed him by the pants, and down the chutes
>   he shot;
> Then turning to Saint Gabriel, he dusted off his hat,
>   Remarking, "That's the last we'll hear of Casey and his bat."

APPENDIX III

STILL MORE SEQUELS, PARODIES AND OTHER TRIVIA

Janet Boyarin Blundell, a library science student at Rutgers, asked me in 1976 for help in locating a parody titled *Casey's Alibi* that contained the stanza:

> I've been against that bloke before
> And put him in the air,
> But when the spitball butted in,
> Well, Casey wasn't there.

I was unable to assist. Can any reader?

In 1976 Frank Perero favored me with four of his unpublished parodies: *Casey and the Boy, Casey and the Ump, The Truth About Casey* and a tribute to me titled *The Man Who Revived Casey at the Bat.*

Kā-Si Atta Bat, by Sean Kelly, first appeared in *Rich and Famous,* a collection of parodies edited by John Guare (Dramatists Play, 1977), and was reprinted in the *National Lampoon* (July 1982) with Rick Meyerowitz added to the byline. Casey, in search of higher wages, has joined a Japanese *basa boro* team where he is known as the mighty Kā-Si. The pitcher first rolls the ball along the ground until it stops dead at the plate. The umpire calls "Stlike one!" The second pitch is tossed toward third for a call of "Stlike two!" An angry Casey throws down his helmet and calls the umpire names. Strike three is called. Having lost face, the bat boy brings out a sword and Casey is executed.

Physicist Leland Herder, in 1979, sent a copy of his thirteen-stanza *Casey at the CRT,* complete with two dozen footnotes to explain technical terms. The ballad is about how Casey, a computer programmer, loses his program by forgetting to copy it onto a permanent disk file.

Illustrations by Tad, San Francisco *Examiner,* 1908

John Shaw, the renowned Sherlockian scholar and collector, sent five episodes in the comic strip *Funky Winkerbean* that ran from October 20 to October 24, 1980, in the *Albuquerque Journal*. The strip featured a football parody of Casey titled *Westview at the Goal*.

Casey at the Bar, an anonymous poem from the *Michigan Gargoyle* (date unknown), was included in Dan Carlinsky's *College Humor* anthology (Harper and Row, 1982). Casey makes a mighty effort to score with a gorgeous female at the bar of a Mudville saloon. The ballad ends:

> He made his moves with sinful style. He looked into her eyes,
> Then let his glance slide downward to her breasts and then her thighs.
> He said, "Hey, babe, I'm Casey, and you'll get to know me well.
> The night is young, and so are you—let's go find a motel."
>
> Oh, somewhere in this favored land, the "chicks" dig "masculinity,"
> And "foxes" for a "macho man" will sacrifice virginity.
> But the woman turned to Casey and she said, "Here's some advice:
> Try *that* line in the minors, slugger—now you've struck out twice!"

Brian Holmes in 1985 sent me his unpublished *The New Casey*. Casey has become a leader in a players' union that plans to strike at midnight. At 11:59, with the score tied, Casey swings as usual on the third pitch, but instead of striking out, he is now out on strike.

Steve Wilstein provided me with a tear sheet of his *Casey at Candlestick Park* as it appeared in the *Times-Advocate*, Escondido Park, California, on July 14, 1985, and in dozens of other papers after the Associated Press picked it up. The San Francisco Giants are playing the Cincinnati Reds on a freezing foggy afternoon with cold winds whipping off the bay. Casey comes to bat with the score 0–0, wearing mittens and a face mask. After two strikes Casey drives the ball high into the fog:

> Somewhere in this favored land, the sun is shining bright;
> Not through the soup at Candlestick, but that is quite all right.
> Somewhere men are laughing, and somewhere children shout,
> For somewhere deep in 'Frisco bay lies the ball the fog took out.

William Safire devoted his October 24, 1985, column in the *New York Times Magazine* to the world chess championship match between Anatoly Karpov and Gary Kasparov. Its account of the match is interrupted by the following stanzas:

> There was ease in Karpov's manner
> As he stepped into his place,
> There was pride in Karpov's bearing,
> And a smile on Karpov's face;
> And when, responding to the cheers,

His opponent he ignored,
Grandmasters of the chess world knew
'Twas Karpov at the board.

"Fraud!" cried the maddened thousands,
And the echo answered "Fraud!"
But a scornful look from Karpov,
And the audience was awed;
They saw his face grow stern and cold,
They watched his muscles cord,
When Russia lost to Fischer,
There was no Karpov at the board.

Oh, somewhere in this snowy land
The sun is shining bright,
The band plays Shostakovich,
Apparatchik hearts are light;
And somewhere children frolic
And Gorbachev's smile is kind,
But there is no joy in Moscow—
Mighty Karpov has resigned.

The third line from the end scans properly only when Gorbachev's name is oddly pronounced, with the accent on "bach" instead of on the last syllable as in Russian or the first as common in English.

In 1988 Joshua Bernstein sent me a copy of *Rendrag at the Bat*, written by his brother Michael, then a Harvard undergraduate. Michael tells how he discovered that the byline for the ballad about Casey's son, on pages 103–04, was actually a name written backward. I am criticized for concealing Rendrag's identity. Critics wonder who Homer was, Bernstein continues, and who really wrote Shakespeare's plays. For the sake of future scholars, he urges me to spell the author's name properly in the future.

Thayer at the Bat, by Robert S. Kyff, ran in the *Washington Post* (June 4, 1988), to honor the hundredth anniversary of the first printing of Thayer's poem. The clipping was sent to me by several readers. It tells in well-crafted lines the story of how Thayer's poem was picked up and popularized by De Wolf Hopper.

The audience arose at once and cried, "Encore, encore!"
They loved the ballad "Casey" so, they begged for more and more.
So Hopper traveled far and wide, intoning Casey's tale;
Soon Thayer's poem made the rounds of every hill and dale.

Wherever Hopper spoke it, there was laughter, there were tears,
He made the poem popular, a treasure through the years.
Still "Casey at the Bat" survives, and "classic"'s no misnomer;
A century later now we know that Thayer hit a homer.

An old-time recording of "Casey at the Bat"
could be heard for a nickel

Two parodies about how George Steinbrenner had been tossed out as owner of the Yankees were sent to me by Ruth Berman. Howard Goldberg's *Casey Steinbrenner* appeared in the *New York Times* (August 1, 1990), and the anonymous *Steinbrenner Gets the Gate* ran in the *Minneapolis Star Tribune* on the same day. The final lines of each ballad are, respectively: "Joy reigns especially in the Bronx—mighty George has been thrown out," and "But there is joy in baseball—mighty Steinbrenner is out."

The Book of Sequels, edited by Henry Beard and others (Random House, 1990), contained *Casey II: It Ain't Over Till It's Over.* Several readers sent copies. Although Casey whiffs on the final pitch, the catcher drops the ball. As Casey speeds toward first, the catcher throws too high, sending the ball into the outfield. Blake and Flynn score, and Casey is safe after a mighty slide toward home plate. The ballad ends:

> But would the fans applaud him—
> Would they scream and wave their hankies
> If they knew he'd played his option out
> And signed on with the Yankees?

"Mighty Casey" striking out, from
a 1901 printing of the poem

Robert Lund sent me Mitch Albom's column from the *Detroit Free
Press* (April 7, 1991) featuring his parody *Today's Casey Finds No Joy in
Mudville*. Casey lets two strikes go by while he and the catcher gab
about the high salaries other players are getting. Incensed at learning
that his forty million (with an island thrown in) is low compared to
others' pay, Casey refuses to play. He sits down on the plate and strokes
his mustache while:

> The fans began to boo and hiss
> How long there must they linger?
> Casey showed his deep concern
> By giving them the finger.
> "How can I survive," he asked
> "On a measly 40 mill?
> If I don't get my way
> I just may join the NFL."
> Finally, the businessmen
> Who'd argued this till dawn
> Sighed that they were finished.
> "Play ball," the umpire yawned . . .

Now somewhere in this favored land
The sun is shining bright.
The band is playing somewhere
And somewhere hearts are light.
And somewhere men are laughing,
But here the money's saved
For justice has hit Mudville . . .
Moody Casey has been waived.

Sherlock at the Bat, by Charles Michael Carroll, came to me by way of Dana Richards. "The outlook wasn't brilliant down in Baker Street that day./Both Sherlock Holmes and Watson found their lives had turned blasé." Sherlock strikes out in his effort to retrieve from Irene Adler the letters and photos that compromised the King of Bohemia. The poem's 32 stanzas appeared in *Wheelwrights* (January 1991), a periodical published by a Sherlockian society in Peoria, Illinois.

Garrison Keillor's hilarious parody *Casey at the Bat: Road Game* appeared in the *New York Times Magazine* (June 27, 1992). Its 18 stanzas tell how much Dustburg fans despised Casey:

Oh how we hated Casey, he was a blot upon the game.
Every dog in Dustburg barked at the mention of his name.
A bully and a braggart, a fathead and a swine—
If only Casey came to bat, we'd stick it where the moon don't shine!

"Two Strikes," by Charles Dana Gibson

When Casey comes to bat for Mudville in the final inning:

> Then from every Dustburg throat, there rose a lusty cry:
> "Bring up the slimy greaseball and let him stand and die.
> Throw the mighty slider and let him hear it whiz
> And let him hit a pop-up like the pansy that he is."

> There was pride in Casey's visage as he took a practice cut;
> There was scorn in his demeanor as he calmly scratched his butt.
> Ten thousand people booed him when he stepped into the box,
> And they made a rich raspberry when he bent to fix his socks.

Casey swings so hard at the final pitch that his hairpiece falls off, and he tumbles over. Dustburg fans remove the lugs from the Mudville bus, attach a firecracker to its alternator wire, smear its windows with smelly cheese, and shower Casey with gravel as he enters the bus.

> Oh sometimes in America the sun is shining bright,
> Life is joyful sometimes, and all the world seems right,
> But there is no joy in Dustburg, no joy so pure and sweet
> As when the mighty Casey fell, demolished, at our feet.

Scooter at the Mike, by Frank Cammuso and Hart Seely, ran in the *New York Times* (October 16, 1993). It retells the famous Mudville game as called out by Yankee announcer Phil Rizzuto, who interjects endless irrelevant asides as stanzas from Thayer's poem are quoted.

"Fanned Out," by Charles Dana Gibson

With a smile of Christian charity great Casey's visage shone;
Hey Murcer, you ever play chess?
A lot of money in that chess, you know. I tell ya.
A lot of money. But it's not a good game for television.
I'm not knocking it, but it's not a spectator sport.
Breaking ball. High and inside. Oooooh.
But Casey still ignored it, and the umpire said, "strike two."

"Fraud!" cried the maddened thousands, and the echo answered "Fraud."
Hey, Murcer! Look! *Bea Arthur!* Didn't she play Maude?
Anyway. Back to Rochester. Gotta get these two runs in.
And they knew that Casey wouldn't let that ball go by again.

In March 1986 cable TV's Showtime presented a 60-minute adaptation of *Casey,* directed by David Steinberg, with a script by Andy Borowitz. Elliott Gould played an aging Casey, with Carol Kane as his fickle girlfriend. Howard Cosell appeared as a newscaster who recites stanzas from Thayer's poem. The plot involved an effort by Boss Undercrawl to turn the decaying Mudville Stadium into a dump site for his factory.

Eugene Murdock's *Mighty Casey* (Greenwood, 1984) is what he calls a "sequel" to this book's first edition. A marvelous work, it contains scores of Casey sequels and parodies that I did not know about, most of them from old issues of *Sporting Life, Sporting News* and *Baseball Magazine.* There are many ballads about how Casey redeems himself with a homer. *His Name Was Flannagan* tells how Casey's liner knocks the pitcher out cold. There are several poems about Casey's son. *The Ball McCormick Hit* describes a home run that wins the game for Punkville and kills a cow in an adjoining field.

Grantland Rice's *Hopper at the Bat,* a tribute to the actor, is included in Murdock's book. Some parodies found by Murdock describe actual games won with home runs by such players as Ty Cobb, Frank ("Home Run") Baker, Babe Ruth and Andy Cohen. There are ballads about actual failures: Hugh Casey, pitching for the Brooklyn Dodgers, loses a game to the Yankees; Reggie Jackson strikes out; and others.

Mighty Casey's Ghost has Casey's spirit rising from his grave to relive the moment of his great shame. Murdock also located a Grantland Rice parody about how Casey drops the football to lose Yarvard's game against Hale. Another Rice poem describes Casey on the witness stand to defend himself in a court case involving his contract.

Sidney Homer set *Casey* to music, published in his book *Six Cheerful Songs: To Poems of American Humor* (1920). *Echh,* a comic book in the Marvel group, featured an illustrated *Casey* in its August 9, 1968, issue.

Among several new printings of Casey, two deserve special mention: *Casey at the Bat,* illustrated by Ken Bachaus (Rand McNally, 1985); and *Casey at the Bat: A Centennial Edition,* illustrated by Barry Moser, with an afterword by Donald Hall (Godine, 1988).

Prose versions giving details about the famous game are *Casey at the Bat,* by Ellen Dolan and Janet Bolinske (Milliken, 1987), and *Casey on the Loose: What Really Might Have Happened,* by Frank DeFord (Viking, 1989), based on his article in *Sports Illustrated* (July 18, 1988). *Casey's Redemption,* by Burgess Fitzpatrick (Greenwood, 1958), is a prose account of Casey's later home run.

In 1986 the Library of Congress issued 7,500 copies of a 1909 33⅓ rpm recording of De Wolf Hopper reciting *Casey,* and sold it along with a reproduction of a rare four-page 1904 pamphlet of Thayer's ballad illustrated by Edgar Keller.

But there is no joy in Mudville—mighty Casey has struck out.

"Casey at the Bat," by Natalie Vermilyea and Jim Moore, in *The Californians* (May/June 1988), defends the conjecture that Cooney, Flynn and Blake, in Thayer's poem, are based on actual players for the Stockton, California, baseball team at the time the ballad was written.

Jim Sherman's "Usury at the Bat" (*New York Times*, October 30, 1994) is a twelve-stanza commentary on the greed-induced strike that eliminated the 1994 world series. The parody begins and ends:

> It looked extremely rocky for the baseball fans that day.
> The Bigs had gone on strike with many innings left to play.
> And so when myriad talks broke down (cajoling did the same),
> A pallor wreathed the foul lines (ain't no "fair" lines in this game).
>
> $* * *$
>
> Oh somewhere in this favored land, things have not run amuck;
> A "catch" is happ'ning somewhere; somewhere the game's not struck;
> And somewhere men stare blankly, and somewhere children gawk;
> But there's still no baseball season—Umpire Clinton hollered, "Balk!"

My good friend Nitram Rendrag has graciously given permission to include here his unpublished parody *Mighty Yeltsin*. It describes how Boris Yeltsin took over after Gorbachev was kidnapped by the Gang of Eight.

> The outlook wasn't brilliant for the Muscovites that day.
> The tanks were rumbling down the streets, the drizzling skies were gray.
> Poor Gorby had been captured, and was hidden, who knew where?
> While a sickly silence settled on the crowd that jammed Red Square.
>
> A straggling few had left the scene, leaving there the rest,
> With that hope which springs eternal within the human breast.
> They thought if only Yeltsin were on hand to take control,
> The Gang of Eight would slink away and crawl into a hole.
>
> And where were Barbara Walters, Leslie Stahl and Bernie Shaw?
> Sam Donaldson was not in sight, nor Jennings or Brokaw.
> So on that stricken multitude grim melancholy lay.
> There seemed but little chance of Boris entering the fray.
>
> No word from John McLaughlin's group: Pat, Jack, or Fred and Mort.
> George Bush was in his motorboat at Kennebunkumport.
> Herr Kissinger was silent. Dan Quayle was on the green.
> Ted Koppel? Forrest Sawyer? They were nowhere to be seen.
>
> Then from a gladdened multitude there rose a lusty yell.
> It echoed all around the town. It rattled in the dell.
> It struck upon the Kremlin, and rebounded from its wall,
> For Yeltsin, mighty Yeltsin, was advancing, brave and tall!
>
> There was ease in Yeltsin's manner as he stepped up on a tank.
> There was pride in Yeltsin's bearing as he gave his tie a yank.
> And when responding to the cheers he calmly waved a hand,
> No stranger in the crowd could doubt, the Bear was in command!

They saw his face grow stern and cold. They saw his muscles strain.
They knew that Yeltsin wouldn't let Joe Stalin rise again.
The crowds are hauling busses now to barricade his door.
The soldiers haven't got the guts to flood the square with gore.

The television crews are there, the radios are humming.
Computer mail is getting out, and Diane Sawyer's coming!
She sneaks through halls with secret mines to interview the Bear.
"I love the way," he tells Diane, "You dress and do your hair."

The Gang of Fools forgot to cut the phones and kill the faxes.
Bush and Boris have a chat. They're not discussing taxes!
John Major tells the Russian Bear to hold the fort and fight,
And even Maggie Thatcher says the Major spoke just right.

No plotter ever got it through his stupid hard-line head
That Stalin, Marx and Lenin, and Engels, too, are dead.
Gorb and Raisa fly back home. The tanks are turning tail!
Boris Pugo shoots himself. The others go to jail.

The Soviet Empire crumbles, but the sun is shining bright.
Shelves may be bare of produce, but hearts are gay and light.
Muscovites toast Mighty Yeltsin, while their children dance and shout.
There is only joy in Moscow since the coup d'état pooped out!

As this book goes to press, more Casey ballads are turning up. Louis Phillips, in the *Elysian Fields Quarterly* (Opening Day issue, 1992) writes about "Casey at the Bank." Its final stanza:

Oh, all throughout this fabled land, where Johnny cannot write,
And schools are overburdened and libraries shut up tight,
The homeless sleep upon the streets throughout this mighty nation,
But there's still joy in Mudville—Casey's gone to arbitration!

Art Buchwald devotes his syndicated newspaper column of July 6, 1995, to a parody about the large sums of money being given to ball players for their product endorsements.

A CATALOG OF SELECTED DOVER
BOOKS IN ALL FIELDS OF INTEREST

CONCERNING THE SPIRITUAL IN ART, Wassily Kandinsky. Pioneering work by father of abstract art. Thoughts on color theory, nature of art. Analysis of earlier masters. 12 illustrations. 80pp. of text. 5⅜ × 8½. 23411-8 Pa. $3.95

ANIMALS: 1,419 Copyright-Free Illustrations of Mammals, Birds, Fish, Insects, etc., Jim Harter (ed.). Clear wood engravings present, in extremely lifelike poses, over 1,000 species of animals. One of the most extensive pictorial sourcebooks of its kind. Captions. Index. 284pp. 9 × 12. 23766-4 Pa. $11.95

CELTIC ART: The Methods of Construction, George Bain. Simple geometric techniques for making Celtic interlacements, spirals, Kells-type initials, animals, humans, etc. Over 500 illustrations. 160pp. 9 × 12. (USO) 22923-8 Pa. $8.95

AN ATLAS OF ANATOMY FOR ARTISTS, Fritz Schider. Most thorough reference work on art anatomy in the world. Hundreds of illustrations, including selections from works by Vesalius, Leonardo, Goya, Ingres, Michelangelo, others. 593 illustrations. 192pp. 7⅛ × 10¼. 20241-0 Pa. $8.95

CELTIC HAND STROKE-BY-STROKE (Irish Half-Uncial from "The Book of Kells"): An Arthur Baker Calligraphy Manual, Arthur Baker. Complete guide to creating each letter of the alphabet in distinctive Celtic manner. Covers hand position, strokes, pens, inks, paper, more. Illustrated. 48pp. 8¼ × 11.
24336-2 Pa. $3.95

EASY ORIGAMI, John Montroll. Charming collection of 32 projects (hat, cup, pelican, piano, swan, many more) specially designed for the novice origami hobbyist. Clearly illustrated easy-to-follow instructions insure that even beginning papercrafters will achieve successful results. 48pp. 8¼ × 11. 27298-2 Pa. $2.95

THE COMPLETE BOOK OF BIRDHOUSE CONSTRUCTION FOR WOOD-WORKERS, Scott D. Campbell. Detailed instructions, illustrations, tables. Also data on bird habitat and instinct patterns. Bibliography. 3 tables. 63 illustrations in 15 figures. 48pp. 5¼ × 8½. 24407-5 Pa. $1.95

BLOOMINGDALE'S ILLUSTRATED 1886 CATALOG: Fashions, Dry Goods and Housewares, Bloomingdale Brothers. Famed merchants' extremely rare catalog depicting about 1,700 products: clothing, housewares, firearms, dry goods, jewelry, more. Invaluable for dating, identifying vintage items. Also, copyright-free graphics for artists, designers. Co-published with Henry Ford Museum & Greenfield Village. 160pp. 8¼ × 11. 25780-0 Pa. $9.95

HISTORIC COSTUME IN PICTURES, Braun & Schneider. Over 1,450 costumed figures in clearly detailed engravings—from dawn of civilization to end of 19th century. Captions. Many folk costumes. 256pp. 8⅜ × 11¾. 23150-X Pa. $10.95

CATALOG OF DOVER BOOKS

THE INFLUENCE OF SEA POWER UPON HISTORY, 1660-1783, A. T. Mahan. Influential classic of naval history and tactics still used as text in war colleges. First paperback edition. 4 maps. 24 battle plans. 640pp. 5⅜ × 8½.
25509-3 Pa. $12.95

THE STORY OF THE TITANIC AS TOLD BY ITS SURVIVORS, Jack Winocour (ed.). What it was really like. Panic, despair, shocking inefficiency, and a little heroism. More thrilling than any fictional account. 26 illustrations. 320pp. 5⅜ × 8½. 20610-6 Pa. $7.95

FAIRY AND FOLK TALES OF THE IRISH PEASANTRY, William Butler Yeats (ed.). Treasury of 64 tales from the twilight world of Celtic myth and legend: "The Soul Cages," "The Kildare Pooka," "King O'Toole and his Goose," many more. Introduction and Notes by W. B. Yeats. 352pp. 5⅜ × 8½. 26941-8 Pa. $7.95

BUDDHIST MAHAYANA TEXTS, E. B. Cowell and Others (eds.). Superb, accurate translations of basic documents in Mahayana Buddhism, highly important in history of religions. The Buddha-karita of Asvaghosha, Larger Sukhavativyuha, more. 448pp. 5⅜ × 8½. 25552-2 Pa. $9.95

ONE TWO THREE . . . INFINITY: Facts and Speculations of Science, George Gamow. Great physicist's fascinating, readable overview of contemporary science: number theory, relativity, fourth dimension, entropy, genes, atomic structure, much more. 128 illustrations. Index. 352pp. 5⅜ × 8½. 25664-2 Pa. $8.95

ENGINEERING IN HISTORY, Richard Shelton Kirby, et al. Broad, nontechnical survey of history's major technological advances: birth of Greek science, industrial revolution, electricity and applied science, 20th-century automation, much more. 181 illustrations. ". . . excellent . . ."—Isis. Bibliography. vii + 530pp. 5⅜ × 8¼.
26412-2 Pa. $14.95

Prices subject to change without notice.

Available at your book dealer or write for free catalog to Dept. GI, Dover Publications, Inc., 31 East 2nd St., Mineola, N.Y. 11501. Dover publishes more than 500 books each year on science, elementary and advanced mathematics, biology, music, art, literary history, social sciences and other areas.